COOKING
the
CARIBBEAN
WAY

Mary Slater

HIPPOCRENE BOOKS
New York

First published in 1965 by Paul Hamlyn Ltd.

Hippocrene paperback edition, 1998

For further information, address:
HIPPOCRENE BOOKS
171 Madison Avenue
New York, NY 10016

ISBN 0-7818-0638-0

Catalog-in-Publication Data available from the Library of Congress.

Cover photo: The Cooks' Festival is a typically Guadeloupean event. Once a year these good ladies parade through town, dispensing from baskets the fruits of their culinary know-how.

Printed in the United States of America.

Contents

Hippocrene is NUMBER ONE in
International Cookbooks

Africa and Oceania
Best of Regional African Cooking
Egyptian Cooking
Good Food from Australia
Traditional South African
  Cookery

Asia and Near East
Best of Goan Cooking
Best of Kashmiri Cooking
The Joy of Chinese Cooking
The Art of South Indian
  Cooking
The Art of Persian Cooking
The Art of Israeli Cooking
The Art of Turkish Cooking

Mediterranean
Best of Greek Cuisine
Taste of Malta
A Spanish Family Cookbook

Western Europe
Art of Dutch Cooking
Best of Austrian Cuisine
A Belgian Cookbook
Celtic Cookbook
English Royal Cookbook
The Swiss Cookbook
Traditional Recipes from Old
  England
The Art of Irish Cooking
Traditional Food from Scotland
Traditional Food from Wales

Scandinavia
Best of Scandinavian Cooking
The Best of Finnish Cooking
The Best of Smorgasbord
  Cooking
Good Food from Sweden

Central Europe
Best of Albanian Cooking
All Along the Danube
Bavarian Cooking
Traditional Bulgarian Cooking
The Best of Czech Cooking
The Art of Hungarian Cooking
Lithuanian Cooking
Polish Heritage Cookery
The Best of Polish Cooking
Old Warsaw Cookbook
Old Polish Traditions
Taste of Romania

Eastern Europe
The Cuisine of Armenia
The Best of Russian Cooking
The Best of Ukrainian Cuisine

Americas
Cooking the Caribbean Way
Mayan Cooking
The Honey Cookbook
The Art of Brazilian Cookery
The Art of South American
  Cookery

Introduction

It was Christopher Columbus who, in 1492, discovered the four great islands of the Caribbean, Cuba, Jamaica, Hispaniola and Puerto Rico together with many of the smaller islands which form a great breakwater across from Florida in the North to Venezuela in the South. Disclosing his discovery to Europeans, Columbus wrote to his king, "I had almost come to the resolution of staying here for the remainder of my days for, believe me Sire, in beauty and conveniency these countries far surpass the rest of the world nor can my eyes tire looking at such verdure."

During one of the coldest winters in memory for most people in England I came to agree with Columbus, as I went from island to island enjoying the warmth and limpid blue sea while searching for, and finding, good things to eat and drink. Some require almost no culinary skill yet will give to a menu just that difference which makes a guest pause, eat reflectively, appreciatively. Others are good for outdoor cooking, giving your barbecue distinction.

Most ingredients are obtainable everywhere and the West Indian specialities are now in shops wherever the people of the Islands have gone to live. The islanders excel in the preparation of shellfish and rice dishes, perhaps for the more sophisticated palate, but many of the fruit desserts and cakes are suitable for children.

Looking at the history of the Caribbean it will at once be understood why there is no one 'West Indian' method of cooking; Jamaica's motto is 'Out of many, one people' and this is true of most of the islands whose peoples migrated or were transplanted from the Old World, bringing with them their habits and customs, their domestic animals, seeds and crops. In the course of time these drove out some of the native plants and beasts just as surely as the inhabitants became integrated into the general pattern. All the islands have mixed societies, the more remarkable because this is the accepted norm and no one sect seeks to oust the others.

5

Cooking of many races is done in adjacent kitchens, many miles from the European, African or Asian homeland.

Columbus found these islands inhabited by Arawaks who, like the Caribs, are now almost memories; yet they left behind culinary words in use in the English language to-day. Barbecue, potato, maize, guava are all derived from the Arawak tongue as well as words such as hammock, hurricane, cannibal and tobacco. These people hunted aguti and iguana, fished offshore and gathered shellfish on the beaches; they trapped wild duck and fowl in a curious way by covering their heads with a gourd (masklike slits cut for the eyes); they then stood neckhigh in the swampy water until an unsuspecting bird passed by near enough to grab by the legs and pull under water until it drowned!

They used salt and pepper to season, their only bread being made from cassava, a root resembling a parsnip, from which poison must first be extracted by baking before it is ground into flour. Neither Arawaks nor Caribs had any of the citrus fruits or sugar products so largely responsible for Caribbean prosperity today, in fact in times of drought, hurricane or hardship 'Coffee without sugar and cassava without salt' is still quoted in Jamaica as a proverbial famine diet.

It was during the Columbus régime that European farmers brought in Old World crops to supplement what they found; vines, olives and cereals all failed at first, rice did only moderately well in wet areas but fruit immediately flourished. Spaniards were partial to their orchards, inheriting some of their skill as growers from the Moors; they brought figs, oranges and lemons from Spain, bananas and pineapples from the Canary Isles and soon no 'Great House' was without its walled orchard and banana trees became part of almost every island scene. Sugar runs like a continuous stream through the history of the islands whose fortunes literally rise and fall with the price of sugar, right up to the present day. It was not until the 16th century that an exportable surplus was produced, again with the help of the Canary Islanders who understood the peculiarities of growing cane which is highly perishable and must be processed almost as soon as it is cut. From sugar came prosperity and, with it, the

6

by-products mollasses, treacle, rum and spirits of wine.

West Indians have been most influenced in their preparation of food by the French and English, both of whom fought hard to break the Spanish trade monopoly and territorial power; the Dutch who, in 1596 formed an alliance with the English against Spain, are the third major influence. Later this alliance broke up and later still, James I, in the Treaty of London, recognised Spanish claims to the Indies. In the Truce of Antwerp which ended a twelve year war between Spain and the Netherlands, Dutch rights were also recognised and it was they who formed the first West India Company.

Pirates come and go all through early Caribbean history; the word 'boucan' means to cure meat by smoking strips over a slow fire. All the islands of the Greater Antilles abounded with wild pigs and cattle, mostly escaped from Spanish settlers' farms; these provided good hunting for shipwrecked mariners, deserters, felons and other lawless characters who became known as 'boucaniers' after their method of smoking the meat that they hunted. As *buccaneers* they were eventually driven into the rain forests by a Huguenot leader, Le Vasseur; drifting back in the course of time, most of the English made their headquarters at Port Royal where they formed the backbone of Jamaica's defences. (Port Royal, a short drive out of Kingston is visited by hundreds of tourists to-day who go there to see Nelson's dockyard). Henry Morgan was perhaps the most famous of the buccaneers, his name crops up time and again in Caribbean history; but, as the islands grew in importance the buccaneers were replaced for defence purposes by disciplined forces under skilled admirals and Port Royal became Nelson's headquarters.

The French, although they lost immense tracts of land and ceded some undeveloped areas, still held a strong position in the West Indies at this time. The Treaty of Paris was the start of a golden age for Martinique and Guadeloupe with plantations producing both sugar and rum in good quantities. But gradually West Indians realised that to rely wholly on sugar crops was too dangerous and encouragement was given to stimulate the cultivation of yams, maize, cloves, nutmeg and cinnamon, as well as coconuts and pineapples, on a very large scale.

Bacon too, grew in importance as hides became a regular export; coffee bushes began to flourish on the hillsides (Jamaican coffee is famous for its mild flavour, Blue Mountain coffee is very delicate as compared with the Brazilian type). In the late 18th century new food crops appeared, starchy foods such as the sweet potato, tree crops like achee and breadfruit became the main peasant foods, while the latter also provided shade for the growers. With the coming of the East Indians and Chinese, rice developed into an item of daily diet; curry dishes with the hot sauces so much used in the Caribbean all stem from East Indian settlers.

American tourist trade has greatly influenced cooking in hotels and travellers who stay in them may think there is no real Caribbean cooking today. Although some were given by hotel chefs, this book does not set out to give international recipes but rather those found in typical island homes and handed down through the years. With each recipe I give the place where I found it, although it may not always be typical of the island in question.

Although the Bahamas and Bermuda are not in the Caribbean, I decided to include some of the recipes and notes on these near neighbours in the Atlantic.

It is not possible to include every island speciality but the collection as a whole strives to illustrate the hotch-potch of customs and the numerous different dishes, some sophisticated, some simple, like the inhabitants of the islands of the Caribbean.

Mary Slater
Kingston 1965.

Acknowledgements

I am indebted to the Tourist Boards on the Islands for their help and to British Overseas Airways Corporation and British West Indian Airlines for the transport facilities accorded me.

My grateful thanks to the many friends on the islands who advised me and to Mrs. Anna Day-Lewis who tested and edited in London while I worked in the sunshine of the Caribbean.

M. S.

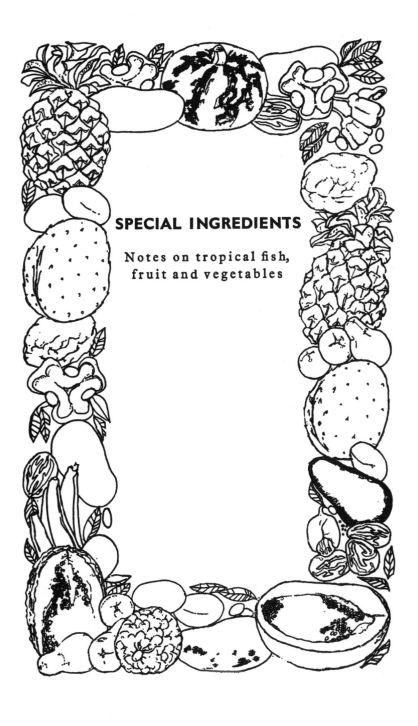

SPECIAL INGREDIENTS

Notes on tropical fish,
fruit and vegetables

Ingredients not easily found all over the world have, as far as possible, been avoided in these recipes; in a few, the ingredients can only be found in the Caribbean.

Tropical fish are easily substituted; these are some which you would eat on the islands besides mackerel, mullet, crabs, lobster, shrimps and turtle which most people know:

Calepeave, like salmon; conch (pronounced 'conck'), a pink shellfish, the meat tasting like lobster; cutlass, a ribbon-like fish with small bones down the sides which must be carefully filleted; flying fish, like herring, grouper, a mild fish like bass, jonga, which are river crayfish; king-fish, like cod, a large white fish often cut into steaks, snapper, like halibut, small white fish with red skins, and tuna, not unlike salmon trout.

Tropical fruit do not, as a rule, travel well although some, well known, are exported: bananas, pineapples, oranges, grapefruit, lemons to mention a few. In the island markets you would also be offered grenadillas and sapadillas, rather larger than passion fruit, soursop and sweetsop, knobbly skinned fruits with a white milk inside, often squeezed into a delicate cream dessert: naseberries which, although larger, could be compared with medlars, a dark, sweet jelly inside the brown skin; mangoes, delicate apricot coloured flesh with a big stone inside a yellow-green skin; paw-paw (or papaya), a big melon with a smooth skin and orange flesh, usually served in slices with a squeeze of lime and very easily digested or used as a tenderiser: there is forbidden fruit, not unlike grapefruit, star apples which are bright red and pear-shaped, with star-like cores, pretty to look at but tasteless unless made into a dessert, 'Matrimony' melongenes are like melons, ortaniques are a delicate Jamaican fruit, a crossed tangerine, ugli fruits are similar to grapefruit.

Vegetables include callilu (sometimes spelt callaloo) which is not unlike spinach; achee, eaten in Jamaica, cho-cho, roughly circular with a green prickly skin, flesh tastes like marrow; christophene a white version of cho-cho: yams, eddoes and tannia, all large edible tubers of the same family: coco — a tuber of the potato/yam family, pear-shaped and varies considerably in size (being starchy, it can be used for thickening). There are two kinds of cassava, one of which is first baked to extract the poison and both are usually ground into flour; cassareep is a hot root; children eat tamarind, a kind of black bean, dipped into molasses as a sweet and it is also used in curry; breadfruit, popular among the islanders, is either boiled and skinned, ground into flour, or sliced and toasted and eaten hot with butter or pickled cucumber sauce, hence the name.

No special utensils are required, but spices should be on hand. Nutmeg, cinnamon, cloves and allspice, a seed resembling the flavour of cloves, cinnamon and nutmeg combined. Creole dishes nearly always require cloves, Chinese dishes often require 'five-spice mixture' to make them perfect (anise, star anise, fennel, cinnamon and cloves, ground and used in equal quantities), monosodium glutamate, made from seaweed, greatly improves the flavour of most dishes; it is now sold in crystaline form under the brand name 'Ac'cent', obtainable almost everywhere, as is the tenderising salt made from paw-paw, 'Meatendra'.

Spice baskets from Grenada are stocked at several stores for about 6/-; West Indian foods are distributed widely, Oriental and Cypriot shops stock guava cheese, tinned mangoes and paw-paw. With few exceptions, almost all ingredients mentioned are generally obtainable.

12

Useful Facts and Figures

Comparison of English and American Weights
and Measurements

English weights and measures have been used throughout this book. 3 teaspoonfuls equal 1 tablespoon. The average English teacup is ¼ pint or 1 gill. The average English breakfast cup is ½ pint or 2 gills.

When cups are mentioned in recipes they refer to a B. S. I. measuring cup which holds ½ pint or 10 fluid ounces. The B. S. I. standard tablespoon measures 1 fluid ounce.

In case it is wished to translate any of the weights and measures into their American, Canadian or French counterparts, the following tables give a comparison.

Solid measure

English	American
1 lb. Butter or other fat	2 cups
1 lb. Flour	4 cups
1 lb. Granulated or Castor Sugar	2 cups
1 lb. Icing or Confectioners' Sugar	3 cups
1 lb. Brown (moist) Sugar	2½ cups
1 lb. Golden Syrup or Treacle	1 cups
1 lb. Rice	2 cups
1 lb. Dried Fruit	2 cups
1 lb. Chopped Meat (finely packed)	2 cups
1 lb. Lentils or Split Peas	2 cups
1 lb. Coffee (unground)	2½ cups
1 lb. Soft breadcrumbs	4 cups
½ oz. Flour	1 level tablespoon*
1 oz. Flour	1 heaped tablespoon
1 oz. Sugar	1 level tablespoon
½ oz. Butter	1 level tablespoon
1 oz. Golden Syrup or Treacle	1 level tablespoon
1 oz. Jam or Jelly	1 level tablespoon

*must be standard measuring tablespoon

13

Liquid measure

The most important difference to be noted is that the American and Canadian pint is 16 fluid ounces, as opposed to the British Imperial pint, which is 20 fluid ounces. The American ½-pint measuring cup is therefore equivalent to two-fifths of a British pint.

French Weights and Measures

It is difficult to convert to French measures with absolute accuracy, but 1 oz. is equal to approximately 30 grammes, 2 lb. 3 oz. to 1 kilogramme. For liquid measure, approximately 1¾ English pints may be regarded as equal to 1 litre; 1 demi-litre is half a litre, and 1 décilitre is one- tenth of a litre.

Oven Temperatures

	Electricity °F	Gas Regulo	°C
COOL oven	225 to 250	0 to ¼	107 to 121
VERY SLOW oven	250 to 275	¼ to 1	121 to 135
SLOW oven	275 to 300	1 to 2	135 to 149
VERY MODERATE oven	300 to 350	2 to 3	149 to 177
MODERATE oven	375	4	190
MODERATELY HOT oven	400	5	204
HOT oven	425 to 450	6 to 7	218 to 233
VERY HOT oven	475 to 500	8 to 9	246 to 260

Note. This table is an approximate guide only. Different makes of cooker vary and if you are in any doubt about the setting it is as well to refer to the manufacturer's temperature chart.

Soups

These soups from the Caribbean are a far cry from the British Brown Windsor; if you like soups at all, you will enjoy some of these more exotic varieties.

The fish of the islands is prominent, the vegetables that abound are put to good use, coconut and ground mixed nuts make just as good soup as do pumpkins and onions. Many of these recipes are intended more as the main course for a light meal, as they are too rich for a first course.

For a small buffet party, a soup such as the fish chowder (see page 20) would be enough if served with plenty of French bread and some good desserts.

These are recipes for experimental cooks who are never afraid to be different.

Bean soup *(Bahamas)*

8 servings:

1 small leek
1 stick celery
1 onion
2 tablespoons cabbage, shredded
1 carrot
1 small potato
1 small turnip
2 tablespoons French beans, chopped finely
2 tomatoes
2 tablespoons peas, shelled
3 rashers bacon

4 oz. lean pork
butter for frying
$\frac{1}{2}$ oz. rice
2 oz. tomato paste
5 pints water
1 clove of garlic
1 bay leaf
pinch basil
pinch chervil
salt
pepper
grated cheese

Clean and dice all vegetables, keep potato separate. Chop bacon and pork into small pieces and fry in butter with the rice and all the vegetables, except potato, until golden brown. Stir in tomato paste, add potato and water. Add garlic, herbs, salt and pepper and simmer, covered, for $1\frac{3}{4}$ hours. Top each serving with grated cheese.

Callilu soup *(Jamaica)*

4–6 servings:

1 small bunch callilu*
2 pints water

1 slice salt pork
1 slice salt beef

Trim the callilu by taking off rough, scaly parts from the leaves, put into boiling water for 15 minutes. Throw away this water and bring 2 pints water to the boil. Chop callilu very finely and add. Boil for 15 minutes then add pork and beef. Continue cooking for 15 minutes before serving.

* Callilu is a green vegetable something like spinach, which could be used instead. It is sometimes spelt 'Callaloo'.

Caribbean nut soup *(Gorda)*

4 servings:

2 oz. butter	1 jar yoghurt
3 tablespoons rice flour or chestnut flour	1 teaspoon salt
1 pint milk	8 oz. almonds or cashew nuts, ground finely

Melt butter, stir in flour, cook over a low heat for 5 minutes, stirring all the time and taking care the mixture does not brown. Remove from heat, gradually stir in milk. Add remaining ingredients, stir well and bring to the boil. Lower heat and simmer gently until creamy.

Gorda is one of the least known British Virgin Islands, still unspoilt and a wonderful holiday island. You get there from St. Thomas taking the boat or the hydrofoil, a service which skims the sea at 30 miles an hour.

Chicken soup *(Jamaica)*

8–9 servings:

1 3–4 lb. boiling fowl	2 slices ginger root (optional)
4 pints water	1 tablespoon sherry
3 scallions, finely chopped	1 tablespoon salt

Put chicken in water and bring to the boil, add scallions, ginger, sherry and salt. Cover and cook over a low heat until the chicken is tender, about 2½ hours. Remove bird, cut meat into small pieces, strain soup and return chicken pieces to it. Reheat before serving.

Jamaica broilers are a thriving business in Kingston where every sized fowl can be purchased, from tiny poussin to large capons. I saw one of the employees wearing a whole chicken as a hat insides scooped out and the rest cured. An idea or do-it-yourself enthusiasts!

Crab soup *(Trinidad)*

4–6 servings:

8 oz. crab meat
½ teaspoon salt
2 tomatoes, chopped
2 teaspoons ginger root,
   chopped (optional)
2 tablespoons olive oil

2 pints chicken broth, hot
2 eggs
2 tablespoons vinegar
2 tablespoons sherry
2 scallions, thinly sliced,
   or chives, chopped

Sauté crab, salt, tomatoes and ginger in heated oil for 5 minutes. Stir in the broth and simmer very gently for 10 minutes. Meanwhile, beat together eggs, vinegar, sherry, then pour into the soup in a steady slow stream. Stir in scallions or chives and cook for a final 5 minutes.

Cream of lobster soup *(Bermuda)*

6–8 servings:

2 pints chicken stock
1 lobster, cooked and diced
2 pints milk
3 tablespoons cream

salt
pepper
4 tablespoons sherry
paprika

Heat stock, add lobster, stir in milk slowly. Add cream and season to taste. Simmer gently for 20 minutes, stirring all the time. Just before serving add sherry and sprinkle a little paprika on each serving.

Cream of coconut soup *(Puerto Rico)*

4–6 servings:

1 lb. stewing beef	pepper
2 pints water	thyme
1 2-inch cube salt pork	2 scallions, chopped, or
2 small white cocoes or 2	chives, chopped
small potatoes, peeled	1 small coconut
salt	¼ pint hot water

Boil beef in water with pork, cocoes, seasoning, thyme and scallions until liquid is reduced by half. Meanwhile, grate coconut meat and pour hot water over it; squeeze coconut in the water to extract all milk and discard pulp. Strain soup, return to the boil, adding coconut milk just as it boils. Stir well and serve at once.

Cream of avocado soup *(Bahamas)*

4–6 servings:

1 onion	1 8-oz. can crab meat
1 clove garlic	1 pint thin cream
2 oz. butter	salt
1 tablespoon flour	pepper
2 pints chicken stock	toast fingers
4 ripe avocado pears*	cheese

Chop onion and garlic finely, fry without colouring in butter. Add flour and stir in chicken stock. Whip until smooth. Mash avocados and crab meat, stir into liquid. Simmer for 20 minutes, then stir in cream, season to taste and heat through without allowing to boil. Serve hot with fingers of toast covered with grated cheese and lightly browned under the grill. Alternatively, chill in the refrigerator and serve very cold.

* On some islands the avocado is called 'guacate'.

Fish chowder *(Bahamas)*

servings:

1 small white fish	2 tomatoes
3 pints water	1 clove garlic
1 leek	1 bay leaf
1 onion	2 oz. butter
1 carrot	1 teaspoon cornflour
1 stick celery	2 tablespoons dry sherry
2 oz. cabbage	salt
1 small potato	pepper
1 small green pepper	French bread

Skin and fillet the fish. Make stock by boiling bones and skin for 1 hour in water. Strain. Meanwhile, chop all vegetables into small pieces and fry lightly with crushed garlic and bay leaf in butter. Stir in fish stock and simmer for $1\frac{1}{2}$ hours over a low heat. Cut fish into small dice and simmer for a further 15 minutes. Mix cornflour with sherry, stir into soup and season to taste. Float bread rounds on top.

Ground nut soup *(Bahamas)*

6 servings:

3 tablespoons ground mixed nuts, or 2 tablespoons peanut butter	3 tomatoes
	2 onions
	1 small aubergine*
1 small boiling fowl	seasoning
4 pints water	6 hard-boiled eggs, shelled

Roast and peel the nuts (if not already ground and prepared) pound to a smooth paste or use peanut butter. Meanwhile cook chicken in water over a gentle heat for $1\frac{1}{2}$ hours. Remove, reduce stock to 2 pints, then, little by little, stir in nut paste. Simmer gently for 1 hour, then return the whole chicken to the mixture and simmer for 30 minutes. Add vegetables, diced small, season to taste, and cook for 30 minutes over a low heat. Just before serving, put in whole eggs.

* Always called 'Garden Egg' in Jamaica

Note:
This soup may be served as a main course with plain rice.
Vegetables may be varied to suit the taste and the season.

Okra soup *(Dominica)*

6 servings:

8 oz. mutton
1 fresh conch or clam
 (optional)
4 oz. white fish
12 small okra
1 lb. potatoes
1 stick celery
1 green corn
1 onion

1 carrot
2 oz. butter
2 tablespoons flour
1 tablespoon tomato paste
 or ketchup
4 pints water
salt
pepper

Mince mutton, conch and white fish and dice the cleaned
and prepared vegetables. Melt butter and cook meat, fish and
vegetables for 5 minutes. Add flour and stir in tomato paste,
blending well. Stir in water and keep stirring until soup
comes to the boil. Skim. Add seasoning and allow to simmer
gently for 2 hours.

Note:
This soup is often served as the only course for a midday
meal.

Okra soup with tomatoes *(Bahamas)*

4 servings:

48 okra, cut into small
 sections
8 oz. tomatoes, skinned and
 chopped

1 green pepper, chopped
1½ pints vegetable or
 chicken stock

Add vegetables to stock, bring to the boil and simmer until
tender but not overdone. Season to taste.

Onion soup *(Bermuda)*

4–6 servings:

2 lb. soup meat and bones	1½ oz. butter
1 stick celery	1 tablespoon Worcestershire sauce
1 carrot	salt
1 bay leaf	pepper
2 cloves	toast slices
1 lb. onions, sliced	grated cheese

Soak bones in cold water for 15 minutes. Cover with fresh cold water, bring to the boil and skim. Add celery, carrot, bay leaf and cloves, season well and simmer gently for at least 2 hours. Allow to stand overnight.

Remove fat, strain stock. Sauté onions in butter without browning; add heated stock, to which sauce and seasoning has been added and simmer slowly until onion is tender but not disintegrating. Pour into a wide topped casserole, float the toast on top. Sprinkle generously with cheese and grill quickly to melt and brown the cheese. Serve very hot.

Note:

The onion in Bermuda is almost a national emblem, rather as the leak is in Wales. A typical Bermuda onion is mild and slightly sweet and at one time represented one of the island's main exports. Today, onions are grown only for home consumption but so synonymous with the Island is the onion that a native Bermudian is often known as a 'Bermuda Onion'.

Orange consommé *(Haiti)*

4 servings:

1 large can consommé	3 cloves
juice 3 oranges	1 orange, thinly sliced

Bring consommé, juice and cloves to the boil. Serve immediately, decorating individual servings with orange slices.

This soup is equally good served ice cold.

Pepperpot soup 1 *(Jamaica)*

6–8 servings:

8 oz. fresh beef	1 green pepper, chopped
12 oz. salt beef	1 bunch kale, chopped
3 pints water	1 coco, sliced (substitute
24 okras, chopped	1 large potato if
1 onion, chopped	coco not available)

Place cleaned and diced meat in water and bring to the boil. Skim and add chopped vegetables and seasoning, then add sliced coco to thicken. Simmer for 2 hours. Serve hot.

Pepperpot soup 2 *(Jamaica)*

6–8 servings:

2 lb. stewing beef, cut up	1 lb. yellow yams
8 oz. salt beef or pork	(optional) sliced
4 pints water	1 coco, sliced, or one
24 okras, chopped	large potato, sliced
1 bunch of kale, chopped	1 sprig thyme
1 bunch of calaloo,	1 clove garlic, finely
or 1 lb. spinach, chopped,	chopped
2 green peppers, chopped	pinch salt
2 scallions, chopped	

Place meat in water and bring to the boil; then simmer for 30 minutes. Add vegetables and simmer for 15 minutes. Then add yams and cocos and more water if soup is too thick. Add thyme, garlic, and salt. Boil until yams and cocos are soft and cooked. Dumplings (see page 48) may be floated in the soup.

Note:
These are *Jamaican* Pepperpot soups, not to be confused with Pepperpot from Barbados or British Guiana, which are stews of the 'pot au feu' type.

    Yams and cocos are obtainable in Great Britain from shops which supply West Indians.

Pork-bone and potato soup *(British Guiana)*

6–8 servings:

1 lb. pork bones	3 large potatoes, peeled
3 pints water	and cubed
1 tablespoon salt	3 tomatoes, skinned and
	chopped

Put bones into cold water, bring to the boil and skim. Add salt, cover and cook over a low heat for 1½ hours. Add potatoes and tomatoes and cook for 20 minutes. Discard bones before serving.

Pumpkin soup *(Bahamas)*

4–6 servings:

1½ lb. pumpkin, sliced	salt
2 oz. butter	pepper
1 pint water	pinch sugar
milk	croûtons

Cook pumpkin with butter and water until very tender. Sieve, then thin with milk to the desired consistency. Season to taste, add sugar and bring just to the boil. Serve with croûtons.

Red pea soup *(Jamaica)*

6 servings:

1 lb. red peas*	1 small piece salt pork
4 pints water	toast

Put peas into cold water and bring to boil. Simmer gently for 2½ hours, then add salt pork and cook for 30 minutes or until peas are soft. Sieve and serve hot with dry toast.

* Available in 1 lb. packets in shops specialising in Indian foods.

Secret soup *(Jamaica)*

4–6 servings:

1 can tomato soup	croûtons
1 can onion soup	parsley, chopped
¼ pint sherry	chives, chopped

Add 1 can water to contents of each can; heat but do not boil. When simmering, add sherry and heat again to nearly boiling.
Serve with croûtons or slices of thin toast with parsley and chives sprinkled on top.

Note:
This is a quickly-made soup which tastes very good. It is intended as a standby for unexpected guests.

Shrimp and cabbage soup *(St. Lucia)*

4–6 servings:

8 oz. raw shrimps, shelled and sliced	2 teaspoons salt
2 tablespoons olive oil	1 medium-sized white cabbage, shredded
2½ pints water	4 scallions or chives, finely chopped
2 heaped tablespoons chestnuts, sliced	

Sauté shrimps in oil for 3 minutes. Add water, chestnuts, salt and cabbage. Bring to the boil, cover and cook over a low heat for 15 minutes or until cabbage is tender but still a little crisp. Serve sprinkled with scallions or chives.

Shrimp soup *(Jamaica)*

4–6 servings:

1 lb. white fish	pinch thyme
3 pints water	strip of lemon or lime peel
8 oz. shrimps	1 scallion
1 teaspoon butter	1 small piece salt pork or
salt	beef
pepper	12– tablespoons flour
2 cloves	lime or lemon juice

Put fish in water and bring to the boil. Boil until liquid is reduced to 2 pints, then remove fish. Pick shrimps and pound heads, tails and skins finely. Add these and shrimp meat to fish stock, together with butter, salt, pepper, cloves, thyme, peel and scallion. Boil for 10 minutes then remove shrimps. Cut into small pieces and leave in a warmed soup tureen. Simmer remaining ingredients for a further 30 minutes. Take out a little of the stock and allow to cool slightly. Mix with enough flour to thicken the soup to taste, return to soup and stir till thickened. Pour over shrimps, add a squeeze of lime or lemon juice and serve hot.

The Jamaica Tourist Board is compiling a Jamaica Cookbook from old family recipes collected by Mr. John Pringle. This recipe was copied from one of Mr. Pringle's pages.

Vegetable soup *(Antigua)*

4–6 servings:

1 onion
1 tomato
bunch chives
pinch thyme
1½ teaspoons ketchup
1½ oz. margarine
3 tablespoons pumpkin, diced
4 tablespoon green peas
3 potatoes
½ small cabbage
3 eddoes (optional)
2 green bananas
1 sweet potato (optional)
water
1 lb. fresh stewing meat
oil
salt
pepper

Prepare all vegetables, dicing or shredding the larger ones. Fry meat in oil, add onion, tomato, chives, thyme, ketchup and margarine and fry until onion is tender. Remove from heat and tip in all remaining vegetables. Pour on enough boiling water to cover and return to heat. Bring back to boil and simmer gently until meat and vegetables are cooked. Season to taste and serve very hot.

Whelk soup *(Bahamas)*

4 servings:

1 large panful whelks	1 potato
1 large tomato	1 oz. macaroni, broken
1 onion	into small pieces
pinch thyme	2 oz. rice, washed
pepper	salt
butter	
water	

Wash whelks in several changes of water, cover with fresh water to a depth of about 3 inches, put the lid on the pan and bring to the boil. Simmer for 1 hour, then remove from water and allow whelks to cool enough to handle. Prise off each cap, remove white meat underneath by piercing with a needle and pulling off. Discard everything except this. Fry tomato, onion, thyme and pepper in a little butter, add about 3 pints of water, the potato, macaroni, rice. Bring to the boil and stir in the whelks, cut into pieces if large. Season to taste and simmer gently for 45 minutes.

Note:

Choose small whelks that are young and tender.

The Bahamas consist of nearly 700 islands although many people have only heard of New Providence where Nassau, the capital is situated. Some of these islands are little more than sandbanks, known as the 'cays'. It was on one of these small 'out-islands' that I was shown how to prepare this soup with many gestures and such phrases as "Look here, mistress, you taka da shell, so, you drop 'm in, so, you make 'm boil-up so".

But I was back in England on a Bank Holiday, thinking how our own whelk stalls could provide all that would be required to make the soup. It may be a long way from Cat Cay to Hampstead Heath, but it's wonderful soup wherever you make it.

Sauces, salad dressings and butters

Sauces are very important in West Indian cooking, especially curried varieties. As in most hot countries, spiced food is popular and hot curry is, in any case, the traditional dish for the East Indians who brought in their own recipes with the first grains of rice.

Salads too are popular and no collection of recipes from the West Indies would be complete without salad dressings.

Where the food is roasted out of doors, barbecue sauce is an essential; sauces to serve with chicken are also important and sauce for fish is something which must be included, as fish, caught offshore and on the lovely sand beaches, is a frequent item on the menu.

Sweet sauces are found at the end of this section with banana, coconut, rum and treacle forming a large part of the basic ingredients.

Avocado sauce *(Bahamas)*

1 large ripe avocado pear
1 tablespoon onion, finely chopped

½ clove of garlic, crushed
Cayenne pepper to taste

Mash pear to a smooth paste and beat in onion, garlic and pepper. Plend thoroughly and serve with any chicken and rice dish.

Note:
This sauce may be prepared in advance if the pear stone is put in. It prevents the sauce from turning brown.

Avocado salad dressing

1 ripe avocado pear
2 tablespoons mayonnaise (see page 35)

salt
pepper

Peel pear and mash flesh with a fork. Stir in mayonnaise and season with salt and pepper. Beat well with a rotary whisk and chill before serving.

Banana sauce *(Tobago)*

2 medium-sized bananas
pinch Cayenne pepper
½ teaspoon guava jelly

1 clove
1 small bay leaf
½ pint water

Peel bananas and chop finely. Bring all ingredients to the boil and boil for 10 minutes. Sieve and serve hot or cold.

Cutting down a banana tree is a very skilled job, the worker has to know just when and where to chop; he wears special clothing as the trees exude a black, rubbery substance. The banana flowers grow on the end of a long, hose-like stalk, purple and sinister. Even in the tropics the fruit is never allowed to ripen on the tree, as the best flavour is always obtained by ripening the huge 'hands' after they've been cut.

Barbecue sauce *(Tobago)*

2 large onions, chopped	4 tablespoons olive oil
4 cloves of garlic, crushed	2 sticks celery, chopped
2 tablespoons tomato purée	2 tablespoons brown sugar
2 tablespoons Cayenne pepper	2 sprigs thyme
	6 chillies, chopped
4 tablespoons fresh lime or lemon juice	1 tablespoon salt
	4 bay leaves

Mix onion, garlic, tomato purée, Cayenne pepper and lime or lemon juice. Heat oil in a heavy saucepan, add onion mixture and cook gently for 10 minutes. Add remaining ingredients, bring to the boil and simmer over a low heat for 30 minutes.

Once you have visited the West Indies you will never forget those barbecue nights with the steel band strumming, the frogs whistling in the scented night. Whenever I make this sauce I have a mental picture of the sea and the moonlight.

Cream sauce *(Exuma)*

1 pint thin cream	salt
1 heaped tablespoon flour	pepper

Stir a little cream into flour to make a smooth, thin paste. Heat remaining cream in a double boiler. When very hot, stir in flour mixture briskly. Add seasoning and cook for 10 minutes. Serve with spaghetti, chicken, fish or macaroni.

Note:
This sauce can be made with milk in place of cream; in this case 2 tablespoons butter should be stirred in when the sauce is cooked.

Great Exuma is reached by a DC 3 of Bahamas Airways, dipping down to land on the little airstrip and off again like a bus at a request stop. Or you can come down from Nassau by mail boat, taking a full 17 hours to get there; and it's such fun, sailing along and singing to the accompaniment of guitars and the lapping of the small waves.

Creole pepper sauce *(Martinique)*

1 small green pawpaw
12 red peppers
1 large onion
1–2 cloves garlic
4 tablespoons mustard

2 tablespoons salt
½ teaspoon ground saffron
1 teaspoon curry powder
1½ pints vinegar

Boil pawpaw in its skin for about 5 minutes then cut into thin strips. Scald and de-seed peppers, then mince or chop them. Mince onion and garlic together. Mix all dry ingredients thoroughly, add pawpaw, peppers, onion and garlic. Stir in vinegar and simmer gently for 20 minutes. Cool and bottlef

Creole sauce *(used on many West Indian islands)*

2 oz. lard
2 oz. flour
2 small onions, chopped
1½ pints stock
¼ pint dry white wine
2 tomatoes (or tomato
    purée)

3 cloves
1 clove garlic
¼ teaspoon or sprig thyme
tarragon and chervil
parsley
nutmeg

Melt lard, stir in flour, adding stock and wine gradually. Peel tomatoes and pulp them, add to the mixture. Add all herbs and a scrape of nutmeg. Cook slowly for 3 hours. Sieve the sauce and bottle in prepared jars. Use with any meat or fish cooked in the Creole manner.

Creole sauce for fish *(Martinique)*

1 small can tomato purée
1 tablespoon stuffed olives,
    sliced
1 green pepper, sliced

1 tablespoon celery,
chopped fine
1 onion, sliced
½ teaspoon salt
dash pepper

Combine all the ingredients. Serve with any baked fish.

Cucumber stuffing for baked fish *(Bermuda)*

6 tablespoons melted butter

3 tablespoons minced onion

1 lb. breadcrumbs

pinch thyme

pinch sage

dash pepper

$\frac{1}{2}$ teaspoon salt

5 tablespoons cucumber, peeled and diced

2 tablespoons green pepper, chopped

2 tablespoons parsley, chopped

$\frac{1}{2}$ teaspoon lemon rind, finely grated

2–3 tablespoons water

Blend all ingredients thoroughly to make a moist stuffing for a fish weighing between 3–5 lb.

Willy Frith is a name everyone knows in Bermuda and Willy is a great fisherman. When he brings in a catch he stores the fish in a tank under his landing stage and they swim around until the time comes to cook them.

Curried mayonnaise *(Galley Bay, Antigua)*

4 tablespoons mayonnaise (see page 35)

1 teaspoon curry powder

Mix well and serve with cold meat, fish or seafoods.

Curry sauce *(Trinidad)*

7 oz. onions, finely chopped

$\frac{1}{2}$ oz. butter

sprig thyme

$\frac{1}{4}$ bay leaf

1 small stick of celery

$3\frac{1}{2}$ oz. flour

$1\frac{1}{2}$ oz. curry powder

3 pints white stock

$\frac{1}{2}$ pint thin cream

Sweat onions in butter and add thyme, bay leaf and celery. Sprinkle flour and curry powder over and stir over a low heat for a few minutes. Slowly pour in stock, stirring all the time. Simmer for 30 minutes, stirring occasionally. Strain, then whisk in cream. Serve with roast lamb.

Devilling spread for fish *(Jamaica)*

1 teaspoon mustard	speck crushed garlic
1 teaspoon Worcestershire sauce	juice of 1 lime or small lemon
1 teaspoon butter, melted	salt
2 teaspoons ketchup or chilli sauce	dash Angostura bitters

Blend ingredients thoroughly; spread on fish just before grilling.
This spread is splendid on crawfish, lobster or cod steaks.

French dressing *(Galley Bay, Antigua)*

juice of 2 limes, or 2 lemons	salt
4 tablespoons olive oil	pepper

Shake all ingredients well together.

Variations:
Add freshly chopped dill or parsley, Worcestershire sauce, dry mustard, or a beaten egg.

Green sauce *(Cuba)*

4 tablespoons sour cream	½ clove garlic, crushed
8 tablespoons mayonnaise (see opposite page)	lemon or lime juice
1 tablespoon watercress or spinach, finely chopped	Tabasco

Mix all ingredients together, adding enough lemon, or lime juice for tartness and a good dash of Tabasco. Whip and rub through a sieve or mix in a blender. Serve chilled with cold fish, especially lobster.
Variations:
Add 1 teaspoon chervil, tarragon or basil.

Mayonnaise

2 egg yolks	pepper
½ teaspoon made mustard	¼ pint olive oil
salt	1–2 teaspoons lemon or lime juice, or vinegar

Beat together egg yolks, mustard and seasonings. Gradually beat in oil, a little at a time, until mixture is thick and creamy; then add lemon or lime juice, or vinegar, a few drops at a time, until the required consistency is obtained.

Mixed salad dressing *(Bahamas)*

1 egg white, stiffly beaten	1 teaspoon olives, chopped finely
6 tablespoons mayonnaise (see above)	3 tablespoons chilli sauce
1 tablespoon beetroot, chopped	paprika

Fold egg white into mayonnaise. Lightly stir in remaining ingredients, adding paprika for flavour and colour. Chill before serving.

Mustard pickle sauce *(Bahamas)*

1 pint vinegar	3 oz. sugar
1 oz. mustard	1 teaspoon tumeric
2 tablespoons flour	

Stir vinegar into mixed, sifted dry ingredients and cook in a double boiler until thick.

Note:

This sauce may be used with any vegetable, such as cucumber, onion, cauliflower, cabbage. Clean and chop the vegetables, bring to boil and cook for 2–3 minutes in salted water. Drain and add to the sauce.

Peanut butter sauce *(Netherlands Antilles)*

6 teaspoons made mustard
2 tablespoons peanut
  butter
1 teaspoon tumeric

2 tablespoons soy sauce
2 tablespoons
  Worcestershire sauce
few drops Tabasco

Mix mustard into peanut butter, add remaining ingredients and blend thoroughly.

Serve with lemon lamb (see page 138).

Peanut sauce *(St. Maarten)*

2 tablespoons onion, grated
2 tablespoons olive oil
2 tablespoons dark brown
  sugar
1 teaspoon lime or lemon
  juice

2 tablespoons peanut
  butter
6 tablespoons coconut
  cream (see page 42)
pinch salt

Sauté onions in oil for 7 minutes. Stir in sugar, juice and peanut butter; add coconut milk little by little, stirring all the time. Stir in salt and cook over a gentle heat till sauce is smooth and thick.

Serve with barbecued meat (see page 123).

Pistachio nut butter *(Grenada)*

1 oz. pistachio nuts
2½ oz. butter

salt

Pour boiling water over nuts, then drain. Remove skins with thumb and forefinger, then pound or grind nuts adding a few drops of water. Mix in butter, add salt to taste and rub through a sieve.

Serve with Lobster Thermidor (see page 108) or other fish dishes.

Pork fat salad dressing *(British Guiana)*

6 oz. belly of pork, diced   pepper
salt   vinegar, lemon or lime juice

Render pork down to extract all oil. Sprinkle salt and pepper generously round salad bowl and pour in oil while still hot. Rinse pan with vinegar or lemon juice, using 1 tablespoon vinegar to 3 tablespoons pork oil. Beat into the oil.

Port Antonio batter for fish *(Jamaica)*

4 oz. flour   4 egg yolks, beaten thick
1 teaspoon salt   3 tablespoons olive oil
2 tablespoons coconut   milk, lukewarm
    meat, freshly grated   1½ egg whites

Sift flour and salt and stir in coconut. Make a well in the centre and drop in egg yolks, working into the mixture. Beat in olive oil and mix in a little warm milk until mixture is like thick cream. Stir in unbeaten egg whites.

To use:
Dry fish well after cleaning, dip in batter and deep fry in very hot fat.

Port of Spain blue salad dressing *(Trinidad)*

6 tablespoons oil   salt
2 tablespoons lemon juice   pepper
    or lime juice   ¼ teaspoon mustard
2 oz. blue veined cheese   few drops rum (optional)
pinch sugar

Beat oil and lemon juice together and mix with crumbled cheese. Add remaining ingredients and turn into a screw-top jar. Shake hard until well blended.

Note:
This dressing keeps for about a week in the refrigerator.

Raisin sauce for ham *(Bahamas)*

8 oz. raisins, seedless or
   seeded
1 tablespoon sugar
1 pint water
juice and shredded rind of
   1 orange

1 small jar of redcurrant
   jelly
1 teaspoon cornflour
   mixed with a little
   water

Chop raisins and cook with sugar and water over a low heat
until thick. Meanwhile cook orange rind gently in juice until
tender. Stir jelly in and heat through until mixture is smooth
and hot. Add raisin mixture and cornflour, stirring. Cook until
thickened.

Salamagundi sauce *(used on several West Indian islands with slight variations on each)*

3 tomatoes
2 onions
½ cucumber
3 red peppers

salt
½ pint water
vinegar

Peel and cook tomatoes till soft. Cut up all other ingredients
finely, sprinkle with salt, add water, vinegar to taste and
simmer for 30 minutes over a gentle heat, stirring all the
time.

Note:

This sauce can be made with slightly different vegetables
but the basis of red peppers and tomatoes must be there to
make a true Salamagundi, in the West Indian· style. The
term 'Salamagundi' crops up in cookery all over the world
and varies from country to country both in ingredients and
preparation.

Sauce Espagnole *(Puerto Rico)*

2½ oz. butter
3½ oz. flour
1¾ oz. fat bacon, chopped
1 onion, chopped
1 carrot, sliced
½ bay leaf

1 sprig thyme
2 tablespoons white wine
2¼ pints rich veal stock
6 tablespoons tomato
  purée

Brown butter, add flour, stirring constantly with a wooden spoon until the roux is the colour of a Havana cigar. Stand until cold. Meanwhile sweat the bacon in a separate pan with onion, carrot, bay leaf and thyme. Cook until golden brown then add wine and reduce liquid by half. Stir this mixture into the cold roux and thin down with stock, stirring all the time. Bring to the boil, then simmer very gently for 2 hours, skimming frequently. Stir in the tomato purée and cook and skim for 1 hour. Pass through a very fine strainer.
If sauce is not to be used immediately, pour it into a basin and stir from time to time to prevent a skin forming.

Note:
This sauce can be kept in a refrigerator for several weeks if it is first reduced by half and then covered with buttered greaseproof paper.

Shrimp butter

2 oz. shrimps, cooked and
  shelled or ready-
  prepared

2 oz. butter
Cayenne pepper (optional)

Pound shrimp meat, blend with butter using an electric mixer if possible. Add Cayenne pepper to taste.

Serve this butter with turbot, brill or sole or any white tropical fish.

Sherwood hot sauce *(Grand Cayman)*

2 large onions
24 chillis
12 tablespoons mustard
4 cloves garlic
2 tablespoons Cayenne
 pepper

8 oz. brown sugar
1 pinch ground clove
2 tablespoons rum
2 tablespoons sherry
2 tablespoon gin

Blend all ingredients in an electric blender and, if sauce is too thin, add more mustard.

Serve with curry or as a mustard. When Sands Sherwood, owner of a restaurant in Grand Cayman, gave me this recipe, he added, "Guaranteed to blow up a safe or a pillar box!"

Spiced fruit dressing *(Galley Bay, Antigua)*

¼ pint orange juice
juice of 1 lemon or lime
4 tablespoons ketchup
dash Worcestershire sauce
 salt

coarsely ground pepper
4 tablespoons mayonnaise
 (see page 35)
2 tablespoons chopped
 parsley

Combine all ingredients and serve over seafood or green salad, or as sauce for a seafood cocktail.

Tomato sauce *(Bahamas)*

2 lb. tomatoes, chopped
1 tiny onion, chopped
4 cloves
1 oz. butter

1 oz. flour
salt
pepper

Put tomatoes into a strong pan with onion and cloves. Cook very gently until juice runs freely and continue cooking, covered, for 10 minutes. Allow to cool. Melt butter, stir in flour smoothly, gradually add cooled tomato mixture, stirring. Return to heat, bring slowly to the boil, stirring, cook for about 3 minutes. Season to taste, rub through a sieve, pot and seal.

Tomato sherry sauce *(Grand Bahama)*

1 large onion
2 cloves garlic
2 oz. butter
4 large tomatoes, peeled
   and chopped

1 bay leaf
salt
pepper
4 tablespoons sherry

Fry finely chopped onion and garlic in butter; when golden brown, stir in remaining ingredients and bring to the boil. Simmer very gently for 10 minutes. Serve hot with lobster risotto (see page 106).

White sauce, classic method

3 oz. butter or margarine
½ onion, finely chopped or
   minced
2 oz. flour

2 pints milk, heated
1 blade mace
½ bay leaf
pinch grated nutmeg

Melt the butter in a double boiler or in a heavy saucepan over a bowl of boiling water; cook the onion in the butter but do not allow it to brown. Stir in the flour, gradually add the milk and bring it to the boil, add the bay leaf and nutmeg with the mace. Allow the sauce to cook in the top of the double boiler for 40 minutes, stirring from time to time until it is about one third reduced. Strain sauce before serving.

White sauce, quick method

2 tablespoons butter or
   margarine

2 tablespoons flour
½ pint milk
seasoning

Melt butter or margarine in saucepan, stir in the flour till there is a smooth paste. Add the milk, little by little, stirring all the time to prevent burning. Season to taste.

Sweet sauces and dressings

Banana rum butter *(Jamaica)*

4 oz. unsalted butter	1 ripe banana, mashed to
4 oz. soft brown sugar	a pulp
	rum to taste

Cream butter and sugar, beating well. Beat in banana, then stir in rum. Serve with steamed puddings.

Note:
Store in a covered jar in the refrigerator or a cool place.

Coconut cream *(Jamaica)*

fresh coconut meat	water

To each tablespoon grated coconut add 1 tablespoon hot water. Stand for 30 minutes, then strain through muslin or cheese cloth to extract all the cream.

Variation:
If using vacuum-packed flaked coconut, add 1 tablespoon hot, not boiling, double cream, instead of water.

This recipe was given to me in 1963 by Violet, the late Ian Fleming's housekeeper, as we stood in the kitchen at 'Goldeneye', his house at Oracabessa.

Hard sauce *(Bahamas)*

3 oz. butter	2 teaspoons rum or brandy
5 oz. icing sugar	pinch salt

Beat butter until creamy and soft, gradually add sugar, continuing to beat thoroughly. Beat in rum or brandy with salt until mixture is very smooth. Chill before serving.

Raisin sauce *(Barbados)*

5 oz. seedless raisins
½ pint water
2 oz. sugar
2 tablespoons West Indian
    treacle

1 teaspoon cornflour
1 lemon or 2 limes
1 oz. butter

Boil raisins gently in water until soft and plump. Drain and keep the water. Mix sugar, treacle and cornflour, stir in raisin water and bring to the boil. Simmer for 10 minutes then stir in raisins, butter and juice and grated rind of lemon or limes.

Serve hot over Barbados bananas (see page 156).

Rum sauce *(Tortola)*

2 tablespoons sugar
2 tablespoons cornflour
¼ teaspoon powdered
    cinnamon

2 tablespoons water
3 tablespoons rum

Mix sugar, cornflour and cinnamon and stir in water and rum, blending well. Cook over a low heat until sauce thickens, stirring all the time.

Serve hot with fruit pie, West Indian style (see page 188).

Sunshine sauce *(Bahamas)*

8 oz. castor sugar
2 eggs, separated
1 oz. butter

flavouring
½ pint double cream,
    beaten stiff

Cream butter and sugar and stir in beaten egg yolks. Beat whites stiffly, then add to mixture. Beat well, flavour to taste and fold in cream.

Serve with any dessert.

Treacle sauce (Barbados)

2 tablespoons treacle	juice and finely grated
1 oz. butter	rind of 2 limes or 1 lemon

Melt treacle and butter and when very hot, stir in juice and rind of lime or lemon.

Barbados is the 'sugar island' possibly more than any other of the West Indies. Field upon field of cane, men and women working together and, saddest sight of all, cane fires which so often send smoke trails into the still evening air. Burnt cane can be used but it makes an inferior type of sugar or sugar product.

Treacle whip (Barbados)

1 egg white	1 tablespoon West India
pinch salt	treacle

Whisk egg white and salt stiffly. Turn treacle into a heavy saucepan and, stirring all the time, bring rapidly to the boil. Tip this quickly on to egg white and beat until cool and light golden brown.

Delicious with bananas, soft fruits or pies.

My driver in Barbados gave me this recipe; he was called Orlando and never have I met such a kindly, courteous man. We spent a week together as he showed me around his island, looking after me like a Nanny all the while. I told him tales of England while he drove me round and showed me all there was to see in Barbados.

Savouries,
breakfast and supper dishes

Breakfast is important on some of the islands, almost as important as in Britain. Bermuda has a traditional Sunday fish dish which you can smell cooking in most homes.

Most of the breakfast recipes would do equally well for supper. Cocktail parties are popular on the islands, always out of doors, often going on till late, so canapés must be fairly substantial and plentiful.

Avocado onion canapés *(Bermuda)*

10 servings (or more according to size of cucumber)

4 avocado pears	salt
3 onions, minced	1 cucumber
dash Tabasco sauce	lemon juice

Peel and mash the avocado pears and mix with the onions, a good dash of Tabasco and salt to taste. Slice the cucumber thinly and diagonally to make longish slices. Dip the slices in lemon juice and spread with the avocado mixture.

Note:
If you make the mixture in advance, put one or two of the avocado stones in to prevent disc oloration.

Baked banana ham rolls *(St. Thomas)*

4 servings:

4 ripe bananas	2 tablespoons flour
4 large thin slices ham	½ pint milk
1 teaspoon mixed mustard	4 oz. cheese, grated
2 tablespoons butter	

Peel the bananas. Spread each ham slice with a little mustard and wrap bananas in the ham. Melt the butter and stir in the flour. Cook, stirring, for 1 minute. Remove from heat and gradually stir in the milk, a little at a time. Add cheese and return to heat. Cook, stirring, until sauce is smooth and thick. Arrange the ham-wrapped bananas in a shallow, greased casserole. Pour over the sauce and bake in a moderate oven (375°F — Gas Mark 4) for 10 — 15 minutes.

Banana bacon breakfast *(St. Thomas)*

4 servings:

8 bacon rashers   4 bananas

Fry the bacon and keep hot. Quarter the peeled bananas and fry quickly in bacon fat. Serve with the bacon immediately.

Citrus kebabs *(St. Lucia)*

4 servings:

[12 streaky bacon rashers   2 grapefruits, peeled

Remove bacon rinds. Wrap each rasher round one or two segments of grapefruit, free of all pith, and skewer carefully, using 4 to each skewer. Grill, turning frequently, until bacon is crisp. Serve immediately.

Cornmeal dumplings *(British Guiana)*

4 servings: (8 dumplings)

2 oz. flour   pinch salt
2 oz. cornmeal   2 oz. shortening
½ teaspoon baking powder   water

Sift flour, cornmeal, baking powder and salt. Cut or rub in the shortening. Make a well in the centre and gradually add enough cold water to make a stiff dough. Knead lightly, make into balls with the fingers and cook in boiling water, soup or stew for 20–30 minutes.

Curried Seafood canapés, Andros style *(Bahamas)*

12 servings: (allowing 2 per head at a party)

1 large lobster or crawfish, or 6 doz. shrimps	toast fingers or dry biscuits
curried mayonnaise (see page 33)	

Remove meat from lobster, shell and de-vein the shrimps. Pound the seafood meat with mayonnaise till it is of spreading consistency. Chill, then spread on toast or biscuits.

On Andros island, where I was given these quickly made canapés at a beach party, crawfish abound. I was asked which I wanted each day, just as if it were milk in England, left on my doorstep as a matter of course! "Well, ma'm", said the fisherman, "you have which you like; de ladies, she haz de weight, de gentleman, he haz de colour!"

Dumplins *(Antigua)*

4–6 servings:

8 oz. flour	2 tablespoons margarine
pinch salt	water
2 teaspoons baking powder	

Sift flour, salt and baking powder and cut in the margarine. Mix to a stiff dough with water. Knead well until soft and smooth, shape into balls and flatten. Cook in boiling salted water for 5–10 minutes. Do not allow the soda to boil out. For those who like waxy dumplins, boil for 20 minutes.

Note:

'Bakes' are made in the same way as dumplins but fried instead of boiled.

Foo foo *(Barbados)*

4–6 servings:

5 green plantains or green
bananas, unpeeled
water

salt
pepper

Boil fruit in water to cover, without salt, until soft. Peel, then
pound with a mortar, dipping this frequently in cold water
to prevent sticking. When fruit forms a smooth paste, mould
into balls, season with salt and pepper and re-heat in the
oven. Serve with pepperpot soup (see page 23).

Grapefruit delight

4 servings:

2 grapefruit, halved and
prepared

4 tablespoons marmalade

Chill the prepared grapefruit overnight in the refrigerator.
Just before serving, spread the fruit with generous helping
of marmalade. Put under the grill until the marmalade sizzles.

Note:

This may be strange to people in Britain but once tried, it
will be found a pleasant change as the start of a dinner.

Grapefruit with rum *(Jamaica)*

4 servings:

2 grapefruit, halved
1 gill rum

sugar

Scoop the pulp from the fruit without damaging the shells.
Place the pulp in a bowl with the rum and sweeten with
sugar to taste. Leave to macerate for 2 hours. Heat just before
serving. Pour back into the shells and serve very hot.

Melon marbles *(British Guiana)*

4 servings as a first course,
12 servings as a party appetiser :

1 water melon	2 oranges
1 gill rum	2 tablespoons sugar

Ice the melon, then cut in half. Remove seeds, then with a scoop (the type that makes small balls the size of marbles) remove the flesh of the melon. Place melon balls in a bowl with rum, juice of the squeezed oranges and sugar. Stand in the refrigerator for at least 1 hour.

As a first course: serve the balls, well iced, in individual glasses.

For a cocktail party: put a cocktail stick into each ball and replace in the melon shell on a bed of cracked ice.

Orange eggs *(Jamaica)*

4 servings:

2–3 oranges	1 teaspoon fresh mint,
flour	chopped
salt	1 egg, lightly beaten
pepper	breadcrumbs
6–8 oz. sausage meat	deep fat for frying

Peel the oranges and divide into segments, removing pith. Season the flour with salt and pepper and dip sections in. Cover each section with a thin casing of sausage meat mixed with the mint. Dip into egg, then into breadcrumbs and fry to a golden brown in deep fat.

Note:
This dish is wonderful, served cold, for small supper parties.

This recipe was given to me in the foothills of the Blue Mountains, among the citrus groves. The oranges had just been picked and there was a surplus, so preserves and drinks were being made to put in store and with the few segments left over, Lena, the cook, made these savoury titbits for our lunch. Eaten among the orange trees, humming birds flitting around, I cannot remember any dish tasting better.

Pork skin chips (Grand Cayman)

fresh pork skin   deep fat for frying

Ask the butcher to trim the skin so it has just a thin layer of fat. Cut the skin into 1 inch square pieces, and fry until brown in hot deep fat. Serve drained, like potato crisps.

Note:
Although I ate these appetisers in the Cayman islands, they originated in Cuba. A refugee gave me the recipe.

Salamagundi (Jamaica)

4 servings:

4 large pickled herrings   salt
1 breast of cold chicken,   lettuce
   cooked and minced   radishes
3 apples, minced   tomatoes
3 onions, cooked and minced   1 hard-boiled egg
pepper

Slit each herring along the side, being careful not to take the cut right to the head or tail, keeping the fish intact. Carefully scrape out the flesh and remove the bones. Clean the fish skin, pound the flesh with chicken, apples and onions, season with pepper and salt. Pack the mixture inside the fish skins till they look full and plump.

Old Jamaican recipes tell you to garnish with barberries and samphire, but failing these, a bed of lettuce and a garnish of sliced radishes, tomatoes and egg are very good indeed.

Salmon Cubano (Cuba)

fresh salmon
½ clove garlic
black pepper

salt
fresh lemon or lime
juice

Cut salmon into ½-inch cubes and put into a bowl rubbed round with the cut garlic clove. Sprinkle with pepper and salt and steep in lemon or lime juice for 12–14 hours. Serve in small scallop shells as an appetiser or cocktail savoury.

This is a 'desert island fish dish' to make when there is no cooker. It is, incidentally, one of the most delicate ways of treating salmon that I know and makes ideal hors-d'oeuvres.

San Juan canapés (Puerto Rico):

24 servings (allowing 3–4 canapés each):

8 oz. bacon
8 oz. cheese
4 tablespoons onions, chopped
1–8 teaspoon black pepper

½ teaspoon salt
½ teaspoon oregano leaves, chopped
12 slices bread

Fry the bacon till crisp, chop finely with the cheese. Add onions, seasoning and oregano. Trim crusts from the bread, toast on both sides. Spread with the mixture and cut each slice into 6–8 squares. Place under a very hot grill until topping bubbles.

Puerto Rico is an island bubbling with life, just as the canapés bubble under the heat of the grill. San Juan is like a small New York, skyscrapers, well lighted wide streets, flourishing, with plenty of smart parties which require good catering and plenty of food and drink. But the old tradition of Puerto Rico underlies this modern re-birth and the spices of the East are linked here with the history of the West, for it was spices that Columbus sought when he discovered America in 1492 and Puerto Rico in 1493. In fact he found none, but his voyage introduced spices into the Western hemisphere.

Anise, corliander, thyme, fennel, sage, mint, rosemary, sweet marjoram and parsley all took root and thrived in Puerto Rico and usually figure in the dishes of the island, which are of Portugese, Dutch, French and Danish origin.

Savoury cheese puffs *(Montserrat)*

8–10 servings:

¼ lb. stale cheese, grated	¼ lb. flour
¼ lb. butter	pinch salt

Cream cheese with butter; add flour and salt. Flour the palms of the hands, roll portions of the mixture into balls about the size of marbles. Flour a baking sheet, place the balls on this, fairly far apart. Bake in a moderate oven (375° F. — Gas Mark 4) for 15 minutes or until firm. Do not let them brown.

Note:

This is a cocktail savoury which is very quickly made for last-minute guests.

In Plymouth, the capital of Montserrat, I walked along the main street by the sea's edge and smelt a delicious baking aroma. I peeped into the bakery and here they were making cheese puffs for a party.

Montserrat is one of the smallest of the islands, it takes only 15 minutes by little air bus to reach it from Antigua. You travel in a shuttle service, six passengers to a bus load; the service is run by L. I. A. T (Leeward Islands Air Transport), associated with British West Indian Airlines. These are some of the smallest passenger aircraft in service.

Sunday morning breakfast (Antigna)

6 servings:

lettuce leaves, washed and
dried
3–4 tomatoes, finely
sliced
1 lb. ling fish, or cod,
cooked and diced or flaked
4 aubergines, cooked and
chopped
2 onions, thinly sliced
1–2 tablespoons oil

3 tablespoons ketchup
4 oz. butter or margarine
salt
pepper
1 tablespoon lime juice,
or vinegar
2 eggs, hard-boiled
and sliced
3 plantains, or green
bananas fried (see page 73)

Arrange lettuce leaves and tomato slices around a large
platter. Sprinkle the fish over and turn the aubergine into the
centre. Fry the onions in oil until soft. Add ketchup, margarine, salt, pepper and lime juice and mix well. Pour over the
fish and aubergine and garnish with egg slices. Serve with
plantains.

Sunday morning breakfast *(Bermuda)*

6 servings:

2 lb. salt cod,
or fresh fish
6 small potatoes, peeled
3 onions, sliced
6 whole bananas, peeled

3 eggs, hard-boiled,
peeled and halved
bacon fat for frying
2 tablespoons olive oil

On Saturday night, soak salt cod overnight (fresh fish should
not be soaked). On Sunday morning, pour off the water,
place the fish in a saucepan, cover with fresh water, add
whole potatoes, peeled, cover and boil for 15 minutes or
until potatoes are tender. While the fish is cooking, fry onions
in bacon fat. Drain fish, arrange on serving dish with eggs
and bananas. Pour olive oil over before bringing to the table.

Salads

Tropical fruits figure largely in the salads and can be bought in many parts of the world; use canned pine-apple, if you must, instead of the fresh fruit whose tartness is ideal for a salad. Lettuce is obtainable on most of the islands, probably im-ported, but there are some recipes which do not require it. In the trop-ics, however, it must be thoroughly washed although in the West Indies it is not considered necessary to use 'pinky' (Condy's Fluid) as in the East.

Avocado salad *(Jamaica)*

4 servings:

2 ripe avocado pears	salt
4 teaspoons lemon juice, strained	black pepper
8 teaspoons olive oil	4 teaspoons rum
1 teaspoon soft brown sugar	4 lettuce leaves

Halve the avocado pears lengthways and remove the stones. Beat together the lemon juice, olive oil, sugar, and a good seasoning of salt and black pepper. Pour mixture into the cavities of each half and run a little of the mixture over the cut surfaces of the pear. Chill thoroughly. Just before serving, add 1 teaspoon rum to each half and serve on a letuce leaf.

When I first saw avocado pears on the tree, they looked exactly like lighted electric bulbs, glowing in the sunlight. In the market, my favourite stall holder, Doris, is always waiting with a few selected pears during the season. "Come on lady, feel up, feel up," she cries and often gives me an extra one as a present which usually means I have been overcharged! But she, like all the other country women in the market, is irresistible, as she smiles and holds out her basket of fruit.

Avocado crab salad *(Tobago)*

4 servings:

2 ripe avocados	1 teaspoon lime or lemon juice
8 oz. cooked crabmeat	salt
4 tablespoons Creole sauce (see page 32)	

Halve the pears lengthwise and remove the stones. Mix crabmeat with sauce, juice and a little salt. Fill the halved pears with this mixture. Serve very cold on a lettuce leaf.

Banana Creole salad *(Marie Galante)*

4 servings:

2 bananas	4 tablespoons mayonnaise
1 orange	(see page 35)
1 lettuce	2 tablespoons whipped
1 tablespoon chopped nuts	cream

Peel bananas and halve lengthwise; peel and quarter oranges, cutting quarters into three sections. Put lettuce leaves on individual plates, arrange banana and orange sections in equal quantities on each. Sprinkle with chopped nuts. Fold cream into mayonnaise and top each portion generously.

Breadfruit salad *(Grand Cayman)*

4–6 servings

1 breadfruit, boiled and cut into small pieces	oil
3 sticks celery, chopped finely	vinegar
1 large mild onion, chopped finely	salt
	pepper

Mix the breadfruit, celery and onion. Moisten with oil and vinegar, using 2 parts oil to 1 part vinegar. Season well with salt and pepper and serve chilled.

Chow chow *(Jamaica)*

4 servings

4 mangoes, unripe	pepper
salt	2 tablespoons vinegar

Wash and peel the mangoes, sprinkle with salt and pepper, cover with vinegar.
Serve with fish or meat.

Note:

During the mango season, the fruit is so plentiful it is hard to know how to use it all. Mangoes often fall from the trees in the high wind before they ripen and they make an admirable salad. At mango time in Jamaica, everyone stops cooking — mangoes become the main diet and people say to each other, "Pot bottom turn up", meaning the pot can be left idle on the stove.

Codfish salad *(St. Kitts)*

4–6 servings

8 oz. cod, or any white fish, cooked, shredded	1/8 teaspoon black pepper
	3 tomatoes
1 large onion, thinly sliced	1 avocado
	2 tablespoons olive oil

Place the fish in the bottom of the bowl. Arrange onion slices on top, sprinkle with pepper. Arrange tomatoes, cut into wedges, as the next layer, placing the avocado, sliced, around the edge. Pour oil over and chill before serving.

Curried chicken salad, Galley Bay *(Antigua)*

4–6 servings

1 lb. cooked chicken, diced	1 tablespoon shredded
1 fresh pineapple, diced	coconut
1 lettuce	curried mayonnaise
2 doz. raisins, stoned	(see page 35)
2 tablespoons chutney	

Combine 2 parts chicken with 1 part pineapple and arrange on a bed of lettuce. Surround with small helpings of raisins, chutney and shredded coconut. Pour enough mayonnaise over chicken and pineapple to coat thickly. Thin mayonnaise with 2 tablespoons boiling water if necessary.

Pickled fish *(Barbados)*

4–6 servings:

2 lb. white fish	3 bay leaves, crushed
1 pint water	2 onions, chopped
$\frac{1}{4}$ pint vinegar	pinch salt
1 tablespoon lemon	1/8 teaspoon black
or lime juice	pepper
6–8 cloves	dash Angostura bitters
pinch ground ginger	1 lettuce
$\frac{1}{2}$ teaspoon mace, ground	green sauce
$\frac{1}{2}$ teaspoon dry mustard	(see page 34)

Simmer fish in water until cooked. Remove bone and flake it, then pour vinegar and juice over, adding enough of the liquid in which fish was cooked to cover. Add cloves, ground ginger, mace, mustard, bay leaves, onion, salt and pepper and bring slowly to the boil. Add the Angostura and simmer for 20 minutes. Allow to cool, then drain fish and stand in the refrigerator for 3 hours.

Wash and drain lettuce, place in the bottom of salad bowl. Fill the bowl with fish and serve with green sauce.

Pineapple slaw *(Bahamas)*

6 servings:

2 eating apples
2 tablespoons green
pepper, chopped
1 small white cabbage,
shredded
1 teaspoon salt

1 teaspoon sugar
2 tablespoons vinegar
4 tablespoons carrot,
grated
6 slices fresh pineapple

Core and chop apples, do not peel. Mix with green pepper and cabbage. Mix salt, sugar and vinegar until sugar is dissolved. Pour over cabbage mixture, sprinkle with carrot and top with pineapple. Serve immediately.

Orange and tomato salad, Blue Mountain Inn
(Jamaica)

4 servings:

4 oranges
4 tomatoes

1 lettuce
2 teaspoons chopped nuts

Place washed and dried lettuce in salad bowl. Arrange sliced orange and tomato in layers on top. Sprinkle with chopped nuts and serve with mixed salad dressing (see page 35) or spiced fruit dressing (see page 40).

Savoury banana salad *(Tortola)*

4–6 servings:

1 lettuce	1 teaspoon chopped nuts
4 bananas	1 cream cheese
1 doz. strawberries	1 carton yoghurt,
(2 doz. if wild)	unsweetened

Wash and dry lettuce, arrange in individual bowls. Shape cheese into balls about the size of marbles, roll in chopped nuts. Peel and cut bananas lengthwise, place in each bowl. Hull strawberries, cut in half and decorate each bowl with a few. Serve with plain yoghurt as a dressing.

Tropical lobster salad, Galley Bay *(Antigua)*

4–6 servings:

1 lb. cooked lobster meat	2 pieces preserved ginger,
3 tablespoons fresh	chopped
pineapple, diced	1 lettuce, well washed

Mix lobster, pineapple and ginger and serve on a bed of lettuce with spiced fruit dressing (see page 40).

Tasty potato salad *(Bahamas)*

4 servings:

2 yolks hard-boiled eggs
2 teaspoons mixed mustard
1 tablespoon melted butter
3 tablespoons cream
few drops Worcestershire
  sauce
salt
pepper
2 tablespoons vinegar
4 large potatoes, cooked
1 large onion, finely
  grated

Mash yolks with a wooden spoon and beat in mustard, butter and cream. Stir in Worcestershire sauce and season with salt and pepper. Gradually stir in vinegar. Slice potatoes and arrange in a glass dish in layers, spreading each with onion, then with dressing. Serve chilled.

Vegetables, rice dishes

It would not be possible, in one short section, to enumerate all the dishes of this type that you might eat in the islands. Rice is a main item of diet and almost every island has 'Peas an' Rice' in some form. Sweet corn is an everyday vegetable and bananas are used as a vegetable all through the islands. Plantains, look like bananas but must be cooked.

Potatoes may just as easily mean sweet potatoes in the West Indies and these are perfect for all sweet and sour dishes. Anywhere that West Indians have made their home is likely to have sweet potato on sale.

Tomatoes are paler and larger, cucumbers rougher and smaller. Aubergines are plentiful and cheap and some of the recipes can be used in Europe as a first course. Okra, sometimes called 'Lady Fingers' can be bought in Greek and Cypriot shops, while Bermuda's onions, are in almost every suitable island dish.

Aubergine baked in coconut cream *(St. Maarten)*

4–6 servings:

1 large aubergine	¼ teaspoon dried chillies,
4 onions, finely chopped	¾ pint coconut cream
1 teaspoon salt	(see page 42)

Peel aubergine and slice thinly. Lay slices in a buttered shallow oven dish, spread with onions and sprinkle with salt and ground chillies. Pour coconut cream over. Cover closely and bake in a very moderate oven (350° F. — Gas Mark 3) for 45 minutes. Remove cover and bake for 5–6 minutes.

Aubergine, Eleuthera style *(Bahamas)*

4–6 servings:

1 green pepper	2 tablespoons olive oil
2 tomatoes	½ tablespoon salt
2 onions	½ teaspoon black pepper
4 sticks celery	1 large aubergine, peeled.

Remove seeds and membrane from pepper, peel tomatoes and onions. Chop all very finely, with cleaned celery sticks. Heat olive oil, add pepper, tomatoes, onions and celery, season with salt and pepper and cook over a low heat, covered, for 30 minutes. Cube aubergine, add to mixture. Cover and cook gently, stirring frequently, until aubergine is tender. Serve with fish or meat.

Banana curry

4 servings:

2 oz. butter	½ pint milk
2 small onions, chopped	¼ pint water
1 dessert apple,	4 bananas, peeled and
peeled and diced	chopped
½ teaspoon salt	4 eggs, hard-boiled and
3 oz. sultanas	quartered
1½ oz. flour	chutney
2 teaspoons curry powder	boiled rice

Melt butter and fry onions until soft but not brown. Add apple, salt and sultanas, previously run under boiling water. Sprinkle in flour and curry powder, stir and cook, stirring, for 3–4 minutes. Remove from heat and gradually stir in milk and water mixed. Return to heat and stir until thickened. Add bananas and cook gently for 7 minutes. Add eggs to curry and continue cooking until eggs are heated. Serve with chutney and rice.

Banana and sweet potato casserole *(Barbados)*

6–8 servings:

4 sweet potatoes	4 bananas
2 teaspoons salt	6 oz. sugar
4 oz. butter	juice of 2 oranges

Cook potatoes in boiling water until just tender. Drain and allow to cool. Peel and cut into $\frac{1}{4}$-inch thick slices. Butter a deep casserole dish and line with potatoes. Sprinkle with salt, dot with butter and cover with a layer of sliced bananas. Sprinkle with sugar and continue adding layers of potato and banana, finishing with banana. Sprinkle with sugar, dot with butter, pour over the orange juice. Bake in a very moderate oven (350° F. — Gas Mark 3) for about 30 minutes. Serve very hot with roast meat, or poultry.

Barbecue onions *(Bermuda)*

4–6 servings

8 onions, peeled	4 tablespoons barbecue
4 tablespoons corn syrup	sauce (see page 31)
or any sweet syrup	pinch cinnamon

Boil onions whole until tender but firm. Drain and arrange in a buttered casserole. Stir together corn syrup and sauce, pour over onions, sprinkle with cinnamon. Bake, covered, in a very moderate oven (350° F. — Gas Mark 3) for about 30 minutes.

Boiled cucumber *(Bermuda)*

4 servings:

2 cucumbers	salt
1 pint salted water	pepper
butter	

Peel and quarter cucumbers and cook until tender in boiling salted water, about 15 minutes. Serve hot, dotted with butter and seasoned with salt and pepper.

Buttered potatoes *(Bahamas)*

4 servings:

1½ lb. potatoes	chopped parsley
6 oz. butter	

Wash and peel potatoes and cut into ½-inch dice or balls. Drop into boiling salted water and cook for 3 minutes. Drain and dry on absorbent paper. Fry in hot butter until golden brown. Serve garnished with chopped parsley.

Candied sweet potatoes

6–8 servings

4 sweet potatoes, boiled	3 tablespoons hot water
2 teaspoons orange rind, finely grated	2 tablespoons oil or melted butter
3 oz. brown sugar	

Slice potatoes lengthwise and arrange in a greased flameproof dish. Cook all other ingredients together for 5 minutes over a low heat, stirring. Pour over potatoes and bake in a very moderate oven (350° F. — Gas Mark 3) for 25 minutes, basting often. Serve with baked ham or boiled bacon.

Candied sweet potatoes, Admiral's Inn style
(Antigua)

4–6 servings:

2 sweet potatoes	good squeeze lime or
1 lb. sugar	lemon juice
⅓ pint water	grated nutmeg
2 tablespoons margarine or	pinch mixed spice
butter	

Boil potatoes, peel and slice. Mix sugar with water, margarine, lime juice, a dash of nutmeg and a good pinch of mixed spice. Bring to the boil and add potatoes. Cook until syrup is thick. Serve with roast meat, specially pork or beef.

Coconut sweet potatoes *(Jamaica)*

4–6 servings, allowing ½ potato to each person:

2–3 sweet potatoes, baked	2 oz. butter
2 tablespoons coconut,	salt
freshly grated	cinnamon, powdered
3 tablespoons beer	nutmeg

Cut potatoes in half lengthwise and scoop out the pulp, taking care not to break the shells. Mash pulp with beer and butter, add coconut. Stir in salt to taste and pile back into the shells. Sprinkle with a little cinnamon and a grating of nutmeg.

Variation:
Sprinkle a little grated cheese in place of nutmeg and cinnamon and brown under the grill before serving.

Chop suey *(Trinidad)*

4–6 servings:

4 rashers fat bacon	4 stalks celery
1 onion, peeled and	4 tomatoes
finely chopped	1 green pepper
1 tablespoon oil	

Chop bacon finely and sear until fat runs freely. Add onion and oil to bacon. Fry until lightly browned but still soft. Chop celery, peel tomatoes and seeded green pepper very finely and stir into pan. Cook, shaking the pan frequently, until celery is tender, about 20 minutes.

Cold aubergine casserole, New Providence *(Bahamas)*

4–6 servings

3 onions	salt
2 aubergines	pepper
2 tomatoes	2 tablespoons
	cooking oil

Slice onions, aubergines and tomatoes in rings and arrange in layers in a shallow baking dish, starting and finishing with onion. Season each layer with a little salt and pepper and pour oil over. Bake in a very slow oven (275° F. — Gas Mark 1) for 3 hours, basting frequently.

    Serve very cold.

Conkies *(British Guiana)*

4–6 servings:

3 large ripe plantains or 4 green bananas	1 oz. conquintay flour (see below)
½ oz. butter	sugar to taste
½ oz. lard	1 green plantain leaf or banana leaf*
nutmeg	
pinch powdered cinnamon	

Boil fruit in salted water till soft, then mash with a fork. Melt butter and lard, add to fruit with cinnamon, a grate of nutmeg and a little sugar. Thicken to a stiff paste with conquintay flour.

Take the leaf, lay it on top of a hot stove till limp, remove the vein and cut into pieces large enough to hold 1 tablespoon mixture. Fold into a small parcel, tie with fine string or the 'shag' or vein of the leaf.

Drop the parcels into boiling water and boil for 1 hour.

* In Europe, vine leaves may be used; they can be bought, fresh or canned, at most Greek and Cypriot shops.

Conkies can be served as a side dish with meat or soaked in oil and vinegar and served cold as hors d'oeuvres. They are even served sometimes as a sweet.

Conquintay flour *(Barbados)*

plantains or green bananas

Peel fruit and slice very thinly lengthwise. Lay slices on a wooden board and dry in the sun for about 4–5 days, turning occasionally. When dry and crisp, pound while still warm. Sift through muslin and store in a tin.

Use for coo-coo, conkies (see pages 70 and above) and bakes.

Note:

I have made this flour with success in England by drying the fruit before a slow fire, then in a warm oven, unlighted.

Coo-coo *(Barbados)*

4 servings:

4 okras	4 oz. cornmeal
¾ pint water	1 tablespoon butter
1 teaspoon salt	

Wash and slice okras and drop into boiling water with salt. Cook until soft. Pour off and reserve almost all the water, leaving about 4 tablespoons in with the okras. Stir in cornmeal with a coo-coo stick*, pressing against sides of the pot to remove all lumps. Gradually stir in remaining liquid, a little at a time, stirring until mixture is thick and smooth. Turn into a well-buttered mould or basin and serve with steamed flying fish (see page 116).

* A wooden spoon is perfectly satisfactory in place of the coo-coo stick, which is a kind of wooden swizzle stick.

Note:
Coo-coo can be made with other vegetables such as breadfruit mixed with cooked minced meat, or cassava, grated and cooked. 'Coo-coo' means a cooked side dish.

Creamed cabbage *(Bahamas)*

4 servings:

1 cabbage	salt
2 egg yolks	Cayenne pepper
4 oz. sugar	¼ pint thin cream or top
4 tablespoons vinegar	of milk
1½ oz. butter	

Shred cabbage and boil in salted water until just tender. Beat egg yolks with sugar and vinegar. Beat in melted butter, pinch of salt and dash of Cayenne. Cook over a low heat, stirring constantly, until mixture comes to the boil. Stir in cream and return to the boil. Pour over cooked, drained cabbage and serve very hot.

Creamy baked cabbage *(Bahamas)*

4–6 servings:

1 cabbage	grated nutmeg
salt	1 small onion, minced or
pepper	finely chopped

For the sauce:

2 tablespoons butter	grated nutmeg
2 tablespoons flour	grated cheese
½ pint milk	butter
2–3 tablespoons cream	

Cut up cabbage and boil until just tender. Chop finely, season with salt, pepper, grated nutmeg and onion.
Make the sauce: melt butter, stir in flour and cook for 2 minutes, stirring. Remove from heat and gradually stir in milk, a little at a time. Cook over a very low heat, stirring all the time until mixture thickens. Continue cooking for 5 minutes. Stir in cream.
Add cabbage and turn into a buttered casserole. Sprinkle with nutmeg and cheese and bake in a very moderate oven (350° F. — Gas Mark 3) for 30 minutes.

Crumbed tomatoes *(Bahamas)*

4–6 servings:

6 tablespoons breadcrumbs	salt
2 tablespoons butter	pepper .
6 tomatoes, finely sliced	2 teaspoons onion,
	crushed or minced

Fry breadcrumbs in butter for a few moments, shaking pan until breadcrumbs are well buttered. Sprinkle a little more than half the breadcrumbs in a shallow, buttered casserole. Arrange tomatoes over, sprinkle with salt and pepper, dot with onion and top with remaining breadcrumbs. Bake in a moderately hot oven (400° F.—Gas Mark 5) for 15–20 minutes.

Cucumber with tomatoes *(Domenica)*

4–6 servings:

3 cucumbers	1 clove garlic, crushed
2 onions	½ bay leaf
2 tomatoes	salt
1 green pepper	pepper or chicken stock
2 oz. butter	

Dice cucumbers, peel onions and tomatoes and chop finely. Remove stem and seeds from pepper and chop finely. Melt butter and cook onions and crushed garlic until golden brown. Stir in cucumber, tomatoes, pepper, bay leaf and salt and pepper to taste. Cover and cook over a low heat for 240 minutes.

Curried rice *(Jamaica)*

servings

½ oz. butter	1 tablespoon curry powder
1 onion, peeled and sliced	8 oz. rice, well washed
1 tomato, sliced	1 pint plus 2 tablespoons
1 teaspoon salt	water or chicken stock

Heat butter and sauté onion lightly, without browning. Add tomato, salt and curry powder and cook until tomato is soft. Add rice and water. Boil until rice is soft and grainy, when all water should be absorbed. Take care rice does not burn.

Fried achee *(Jamaica)*

achee*	butter
salt water	

Discard seeds and pink skin from the cream-coloured achee flesh. Cover with salt water (1 tablespoon salt to 1 pint water), for 5 minutes. Drain and fry in hot butter.

* Canned achee is available in Great Britain

Note:

Can also be coated in batter before frying, to make achee fritters. Make the batter of flour, salt, egg and milk.

Achee is almost a national dish in Jamaica where it is so plentiful that it could almost be counted as 'free' food. It grows on trees and looks like a large green or yellow plum before it bursts to disclose three shiny black seeds inside. If eaten before it is ripe, it is poisonous. Fried achee is often served as an appetiser.

Fried okra *(Bahamas)*

okra
breadcrumbs

deep fat for frying

Slice okra pods about 1/8 inch thick, dip into breadcrumbs and fry in hot fat.

Note:

For 'French fried okra', use only young pods, parboiled whole, dipped in a batter made of flour, salt, egg and milk, then fried.

Fried plantains *(Bermuda)*

plantains
flour

powdered cinnamon
butter

Slice plantains in three, lengthwise. Dust with flour flavoured with a little cinnamon and fry quickly in hot butter until golden brown.

Note:

Green bananas may be used in place of plantains.

Fried rice, Chow fan *(Trinidad)*

4–6 servings:

1 lb. rice, well-washed
water
salt
4 tablespoons oil
6-8 oz. cooked pork,
  chicken, shrimp, ham or
  lobster

4 tablespoons scallions or
  spring onions, finely
  chopped
pinch pepper
2 eggs, lightly beaten
3 tablespoons parsley,
  finely chopped
soy sauce

Cook rice in plenty of salted water, drain thoroughly and refrigerate for 12 hours. Heat oil and fry rice in it, stirring, until golden brown. Stir in pork, scallions, salt, and pepper. Cook for 1 minute, stirring. Make a well in the centre, and pour eggs in. Cook until eggs begin to set, then stir thoroughly. Stir in parsley and soy sauce to taste and serve hot.

Grilled corn-on-the-cob *(Jamaica)*

young corn cobs   butter or fresh cream

Choose very fresh and young corn cobs and grill under a gentle heat, basting frequently with butter. Do not add salt. When cobs are swollen and golden brown, serve, passing melted butter or fresh cream separately.

Hoppin' John *(Bahamas)*

4 servings:

3–4 rashers fat bacon,
  finely chopped
1 large onion
4 tomatoes, peeled
1½ pints water

8 oz. dried peas, boiled
  until very tender
8 oz. rice, well washed
salt
pepper

Sweat bacon and fry chopped onion and tomatoes in it until golden brown. Stir in peas, rice and water. Season with salt and pepper, return to the boil and cook slowly until rice is tender and all water absorbed.

A little more water may be added if it dries out before the rice is tender but the final dish should be dry and fluffy. An occasional stir during cooking will prevent sticking.

Note:

This is the traditional 'peas an' rice' of the Bahamas but beans may be used instead of peas.

Jug-jug *(Barbados)*

4–6 servings:

1 lb. split peas, soaked	water
8 oz. lean pork or salt beef (or 4 oz. each)	5 oz. cornflour
1 small onion, chopped	salt
2 or 3 blades of chive, chopped	pepper

Cut up meat, season and stew with onions and chives in 1½ pints water for about 20 minutes (if salt beef is used it should first be soaked). Add peas and stew for a further 30 minutes or until the peas are soft. Strain off, retain 1 pint liquid. Mince or chop meat and peas. To ½ pint liquid, add meat and peas, stir in cornflour. Cook for 20–30 minutes stirring all the time, add extra liquid if necessary. The mixture should be like a paste; put into a buttered basin and serve hot.

Note:

Jug-jug, similar to pease pudding, is a traditional Christmas dish in Barbados.

Kidney beans and pork, Nassau style *(Bahamas)*

4 servings:

1 lb. kidney beans	1 tablespoon
8 oz. salt pork, chopped	Worcestershire sauce
1 onion, finely chopped	salt
2 tablespoons vinegar	black pepper
	3 oz. soft brown sugar

Wash beans and soak for 2 hours in cold water. Drain, cover with fresh, unsalted water and boil gently until tender. Cut pork into small pieces and pile into centre of a large baking pan. Mix beans and liquid in which they were cooked with remaining ingredients. Add a little more water if necessary so that the mixture will not dry out during the long baking. Surround pork with mixture and bake, uncovered, in a very moderate oven (350°F. — Gas Mark 3) for 2½ hours, when the ingredients should have thickened. Stir occasionally with a wooden spoon to prevent sticking.

Mixed vegetable platter or 'gado-gado' *(Surinam)*

4–6 servings:

1 cabbage	4 oz. bean sprouts
1 lb. green beans	1 tomato, finely sliced
water	2 eggs, hard-boiled and
1 cucumber	finely sliced
1 aubergine	

Chop cabbage and simmer in water with beans cut in short lengths. Peel and dice cucumber and aubergine. Add with bean sprouts to cabbage and beans and cook. When tender, drain and arrange attractively on a large platter with tomato and egg. Serve hot, or cold with peanut sauce (see page 36), arranged on a bed of cos lettuce.

In Paramaribe, an old Dutch town in Surinam, you will see Javanese, Amer-Indians, Creoles, Chinese, Hindus and Bush

Negroes all rubbing shoulders in the market place and shops. The town has modern hotels but just around the corner is the primitive life of the native villages and you travel by dugout canoe at night to watch the fire dancers.

Surinam River runs through Paramaribe, packed with all kinds of colourful river craft and you almost feel you are in the East rather than the Caribbean. Surinam is not as yet well known but is a very good place for a holiday.

Nasi Goreng (An Indonesian dish served in the Netherlands Antilles)

4 servings:

8 oz. rice	clove of garlic, chopped
water	4 prawns (more if very
1 chicken breast	small)
4 oz. chicken liver	salt
2 oz. rump steak	pepper
4 tablespoons peanut oil	3 large tomatoes, sliced
3 spring onions, finely	½ cucumber, sliced
chopped, stalks included	1 large onion, sliced

Wash and drain rice, cover with 2 inches water and boil with the lid on until water is absorbed. Lower heat and simmer very gently till rice is dry and fluffy.

While rice is cooking, cut up chicken liver and steak, and fry in oil with spring onions, garlic and prawns. Mix in cooked rice, season with salt and pepper and fry over a low heat till all the ingredients are well blended. Turn on to a large serving dish and decorate with slices of tomato, cucumber and golden fried onion.

Onion cheese *(Bermuda)*

4–6 servings:

6 onions
4 eggs
2 oz. butter
4 thick slices wholemeal
   bread

3 oz. grated cheese
¼ pint milk
pinch salt
pepper

Peel onions and cover with cold water. Bring to the boil and cook for 3 minutes. Drain and cool, then cut in ½-inch thick slices. Toast bread, cut each slice in half and arrange in a well-buttered casserole. Cover with onion slices, sprinkle with cheese. Beat eggs with milk, salt and pepper and pour over onions. Dot with butter and bake in a very moderate oven (350°F. — Gas Mark 3) for about 30 minutes.

Onions baked in cream *(Bermuda)*

4 servings:

4 onions
½ teaspoon salt

4 tablespoons fresh cream

Peel onions and slice thinly. Arrange in a buttered, shallow dish, sprinkle with salt and pour cream over. Bake in a very moderate oven (350°F. — Gas Mark 3) for 20–25 minutes until onions are tender.

Paprika potatoes *(Bermuda)*

4 servings:

4 large potatoes, peeled
   and diced
2 oz. butter
1 small onion, finely sliced

1 teaspoon paprika
salt
¼ pint water

Dry potato dice in a cloth or absorbent paper. Heat butter, add potatoes, onion and paprika and salt to taste. Lower heat and cook very gently for 6 or 7 minutes, shaking pan occasionally to turn vegetables. Bring water to the boil, pour over vegetables, cover closely and cook gently for 15 minutes, until potatoes and onions are tender and all water absorbed.

Peas an' rice *(Jamaica)*

4–6 servings:

8 oz. split peas	1 clove garlic
2 pints water	2 blades chive, chopped
½ teaspoon bicarbonate of soda	sprig thyme, chopped
	sprig parsley, chopped
8 oz. soup meat, optional	1 tomato, peeled and
12 oz. rice, washed	chopped
1 small onion, chopped	⅛ teaspoon black pepper
1 oz. lard	1 teaspoon salt

Pick and wash peas, soak in 1 pint water and bicarbonate of soda overnight. Wash and cut up meat. Simmer with peas and garlic in water in which peas were soaked. Brown onion, tomato, parsley, chives and thyme in lard, add to meat and peas. When peas are nearly soft, but not disintegrating, add rice which has been cooked separately in remaining water. Season with salt and pepper.

Peas and rice with ham *(Trinidad)*

4 servings:

8 oz. dried split peas, well soaked	4 oz. raw ham, chopped
	salt
8 oz. rice	pepper

Cover peas with 1 pint water, bring to the boil and simmer until soft, about 30 minutes. Cook rice in ¾ pint boiling, salted water for 15 minutes. Cook ham in ½ pint water for 15–20 minutes. Drain all ingredients, add peas and ham to rice. Season to taste.

Potato cakes *(Bahamas)*

4–6 servings:

2 lb. potatoes	pepper
2 oz. butter	breadcrumbs
1 egg, lightly beaten	fat
salt	

Peel potatoes, boil until tender and mash smoothly with butter and egg. Season to taste. Allow to cool. Shape into small cakes, press into breadcrumbs and fry in hot fat.

Variations:

A little cream or milk may be added to the mashed potato; mash 4 oz. grated cheese into the potato while it is hot.

Potato puff *(Bermuda)*

4–6 servings:

2 lb. potatoes	salt
2 eggs, separated	pepper
1 small onion	butter

Peel potatoes, boil until tender and mash thoroughly. Stir in well-beaten egg yolks and crushed or minced onion. Season to taste and fold in stiffly beaten egg whites. Pile high in a shallow, buttered casserole and bake for about 20 minutes in a very moderate oven (350° F. — Gas Mark 3).

Rice pilaff *(Trinidad)*

4–6 servings:

8 oz. rice	sprig parsley, chopped
1 small onion, chopped	sprig thyme, chopped
$\frac{1}{2}$ oz. butter	salt
2 pints water or chicken stock	pepper

Sweat onion in ¼ oz. butter, add rice, sweating this also. Stir until rice is well fried but not brown. Pour water over, add parsley, thyme, salt and pepper, cover and cook over a gentle heat for 20 minutes. Drain rice, put into a clean saucepan, add remaining butter in tiny pieces and separate grains with a fork.

Note:

For Indian style rice, add 1 tablespoon curry powder to the cooked rice. For rice cooked with sweet green peppers, often eaten in the West Indies, blanch peppers by dipping into boiling water, remove seeds, dice and cook with rice.

Rice and raisin croquettes *(Tobago)*

4–6 servings:

2 oz. rice	2 oz. butter
1 pint water	yolk of 2 eggs
½ pint plus 1 tablespoon milk	1 oz. raisins, stoned and washed
1 small onion stuck with cloves	flour
pinch salt	breadcrumbs

Put rice in an ovenproof dish with water; bring to the boil and boil for 3 minutes. Wash and rinse rice under a running tap. Boil ½ pint milk and return rice with milk to dish. Add onion, ½ oz. butter and salt. Cook in a very moderate oven (350° F. — Gas Mark 3) for 30 minutes.

Take from the oven and remove the onion, add ½ oz. butter cut in small pieces, beat egg yolks with remaining milk, retaining about a quarter of the egg yolk. Stir beaten egg and milk into rice mixture, then add raisins, stirring again. Butter a very shallow baking tin, pour in mixture and allow to become cold.

Cut into squares, dip into flour, then egg and bread crumbs. Fry in remaining butter until brown on all sides.

Note:

These croquettes are good with any meat.

Savoury baked bananas *(Charlotte Amalie)*

4 servings:

4 bananas	salt
butter	pepper

Bake unpeeled bananas until the skins split open, about 20 minutes, in a very moderate oven (350° F. — Gas Mark 3). Peel, brush bananas with melted butter, sprinkle with salt and pepper. Serve as a vegetable or garnish, particularly for Chicken Maryland (see page 129).

Scalloped okra with tomatoes *(Bahamas)*

4–6 servings:

1 oz. butter	6 medium-sized okra, boiled
1 oz. flour	4 tomatoes, finely chopped
½ pint milk	
salt	
pepper	4 tablespoons breadcrumbs
sprig thyme	

Melt butter, stir in flour and cook, stirring for 2 minutes. Remove from heat and gradually stir in milk. Return to heat and bring to the boil, stirring. Season with salt, pepper and thyme and cook over a low heat for 5 minutes. Chop okra, mix in tomatoes and most of the breadcrumbs and turn into buttered shallow baking. pan. Season and cover with sauce. Sprinkle with remaining breadcrumbs, bake in a moderate (375° F. — Gas Mark 4) for 15 minutes.

Stewed pumpkin *(Jamaica)*

4–6 servings:

2 lb. pumpkin	¼ pint cold milk
½ pint hot water	1 teaspoon cinnamon
½ teaspoon salt	pepper
½ oz. butter	½ pint hot water
½ oz. flour	

Peel pumpkin and remove seeds; cut into 1-inch strips. Place in double saucepan with water, salt and butter. Cover, cook until tender. Drain and place in heated dish, keeping the liquid. Mix flour with milk to a smooth paste, pour pumpkin water over. Return to pan and boil, stirring all the time. Season with pepper and cinnamon, then pour over pumpkin.

Stuffed aubergine (*Jamaica*)

4 servings:

2 large aubergines	pepper
3 oz. butter	4 tablespoons cashew nuts,
4 oz. cooked meat, minced	finely chopped
salt	breadcrumbs

Cut aubergines in half lengthwise, scoop out pulp taking care not to damage skins. Chop pulp and sweat gently in 1½ oz. butter until tender. Turn into a bowl with meat, season with plenty of salt and pepper. Stir in cashew nuts and mix with remaining butter, melted. Pile into aubergine skins, sprinkle with breadcrumbs and bake in a shallow, greased pan in a very moderate oven (350° F. — Gas Mark 3), for 25 minutes.

Stuffed avocado pears, Chef Anthony style
(*Bahamas*)

4 servings:

1 small can crabmeat	1 tablespoon olive oil
2 ripe avocado pears	½ teaspoon sugar
small onion, finely chopped	pinch salt
1 teaspoon vinegar	pepper

Mix crabmeat with onion, oil, vinegar, salt, pepper and sugar. Split avocados lengthwise, remove stones and stuff with mixture. Chill before serving.

Stuffed breadfruit *(Trinidad)*

4 servings:

2 large breadfruit	1 small onion, finely
8 oz. fresh beef or pork	chopped
4 oz. salt beef or pork	few chives, chopped
1 thick slice raw ham	salt
1 oz. butter or margarine	pepper
1 tomato, chopped	butter

Peel breadfruit and parboil whole, in salted water. Mince meats and fry in butter until browned. Stir in tomato, onion and chives, season to taste. Score cooled breadfruit and cut core out and a little flesh from the stalk end. Pack with stuffing and bake in a very moderate oven (350° F. — Gas Mark 3) until soft and brown, about 45 minutes.
Serve spread with a little butter.

Note:

Breadfruit is not very tasty unless cooked with highly flavoured ingredients. It can be fried or creamed, like potato, if well seasoned.

Stuffed green peppers and tomatoes *(Trinidad)*

4 servings:

4 large green peppers

For the stuffing:

2 tablespoons cooking oil	salt
3 tablespoons onion,	paprika pepper
minced	3 tablespoons cooked beef,
4 tablespoons cooked rice	minced finely
rind of 1 lemon, grated	4 tomatoes, finely sliced

Cover peppers with cold water, bring to the boil and simmer gently until tender but still firm. Drain and allow to cool. *Make the stuffing:* heat oil and fry onion until golden brown. Add rice, lemon rind, a good pinch of salt and paprika pepper and beef. Stir over a low heat until warmed through.

Slice off tops of peppers and carefully scoop out seeds and membranes. Pack in stuffing, arrange in a greased baking tin and surround with tomatoes. Bake in a moderate oven (375°F. — Gas Mark 4) for about 20 minutes.

Stuffed tomatoes *(Bahamas)*

4 servings:

4 large firm tomatoes	pepper
1 tablespoon breadcrumbs	1 small onion, crushed or
1 tablespoon cooked	minced
chicken, finely chopped	½ oz. butter
salt	

Cut a slice from the stem end of the tomatoes, scoop out seeds and pulp. Chop pulp and mix in breadcrumbs and chicken. Season to taste, add onion. Sprinkle a little salt into tomato shells, pack with stuffing, top each with 1 teaspoon butter and arrange in a greased pan. Bake in a moderately hot oven (400°F. — Gas Mark 5) for about 20 minutes.

Sweet cucumber *(Bermuda)*

4 servings:

2 cucumbers	sprig parsley, finely
4 teaspoons sugar	chopped
2 tablespoons vinegar	salt

Peel cucumber and slice very thinly. Arrange in a shallow dish, sprinkle with sugar and vinegar. Chill and, just before serving sprinkle with parsley and a little salt.

Sweet potatoes baked in oranges *(Bahamas)*

6 servings:

6 sweet potatoes	2 teaspoons grated orange
salted water	peel
6 oranges	2 tablespoons orange juice
4 tablespoons cream	2 tablespoons sugar
2 oz. butter	salt

Wash potatoes, boil in salted water until tender, drain and peel. Mash thoroughly. Slice tops off oranges, carefully scoop out all flesh. Beat cream, butter, orange peel and juice, sugar and a good pinch salt into potatoes. Fill orange shells with this. Bake in a moderate oven (350° F. — Gas Mark 4) until nicely browned on top, about 20 minutes.

Topped tomatoes, New Providence style *(Bahamas)*

4 servings:

4 small potatoes	salt
salted water	2 very large tomatoes
1 tablespoon milk	4 teaspoons cheese, grated
2 teaspoons butter	paprika

Peel potatoes, boil in salted water until tender. Mash with milk and butter, adding salt if necessary. Beat until creamy and smooth. Halve tomatoes and pile high with the creamed potato. Cover with grated cheese and a sprinkling of paprika. Arrange in an oven-proof dish with a little water in the bottom. Bake in a moderately hot oven (400° F. — Gas Mark 5) on a low shelf, for 15–20 minutes.

Fish dishes

Fish is one of the most important items of diet on the islands where it is both plentiful and much cheaper than meat. No island is without its fish speciality, fish are there to be picked up on the beaches, lobster, crayfish, crawfish, crabs and shrimps in abundance.

I never realised the true meaning of 'shell pink' until I saw the conchs on the beach at Grand Cayman, seven miles of perfect white sands, and the shells coming in on every tide, some satiny palest pink, others polished magenta.

You may not find conch, or even turtle, in your part of the globe but there will almost certainly be lobster or crab. Flying fish you may never see but whiting, herring and mackerel will be there; grouper, snapper and king fish are tropical fish of the islands but, in all the recipes, a similar white fish is given as an alternative.

If you do not like fish cooked entirely in the Creole manner, a Creole sauce enlivens the plainest fish dish: you need not follow the recipes faithfully but be inspired by the islanders who know better than anyone how best to prepare their fish.

In Bermuda you may hear on the radio 'Get your jacks at the flag pole' which means that a catch of mackerel is in and on sale at the flag pole down by the dock. On the smaller islands you will hear the conch horn blow, which means the fish boat is in, good news for the islanders.

In the tropics, limes are more plentiful than lemons but in every recipe where lime juice is mentioned, lemon may be substituted.

Baked black crabs *(Jamaica)*

4 servings:

6 black crabs, boiled	pinch Cayenne
1½ tablespoons butter, melted	pinch nutmeg
	salt
½ teaspoon black pepper	breadcrumbs
1 teaspoon vinegar	butter

Carefully pick all meat from claws and smaller bones. Open the backs, extract eggs, throw away the gall and reserve the black water. Mix meat with butter, pepper, vinegar, cayenne and nutmeg, add salt to taste. Pack into 4 of the well-washed shells sharing the black water between them and adding 1–2 eggs to each shell. Sprinkle well with breadcrumbs, dot with butter and brown in a hot oven (425°F. — Gas Mark 6).

Baked crabs *(Bahamas)*

6 servings:

6 crabs, boiled	1 egg, lightly beaten
4 oz. breadcrumbs	1 oz. butter, melted
1 onion, finely chopped	salt
1 stick celery, finely chopped	pepper
2 tomatoes, finely chopped	pinch thyme

Pick the crabs and claws, and clean the shells. Flake crab meat and stir with remaining ingredients. Return to shell backs and bake in a moderate oven (375°F. — Gas Mark 4) for about 15 minutes.

Baked fish, Bemuda style

4–6 servings:

1 4-lb. fish	bacon rashers
cucumber stuffing (see page 33)	lemon pieces
melted butter	1 stuffed olive
3 tablespoons lemon juice	devilling spread (see page 34)

Wash fish and slit open to the tail. Clean and stuff, then sew or skewer together. Place the fish on a piece of aluminium foil in a shallow baking dish. Wrap the head and tail in foil to prevent burning. Brush the rest of the fish with melted butter, pour over lemon juice and lay bacon rashers over the fish.

Bake, uncovered in a hot oven (425°F. — Gas Mark 6) for 12 minutes to the pound. Remove foil and carefully place fish on a heated dish. Garnish with lemon pieces and place a stuffed olive in the eye. Serve with devilling spread.

Baked fresh fish, British Honduras style

4 servings:

1 lb. fish	pinch pepper
salt	1 oz. butter, melted
pepper	2 oz. fat pork, sliced
4 tablespoons fresh	3 oz. butter
breadcrumbs	3 tablespoons vinegar
¼ onion, minced	2 tomatoes, sliced
1 teaspoon vinegar	1 large onion, sliced

Clean fish, rinse and dry it. Rub with salt and pepper. Prepare a stuffing by mixing breadcrumbs with minced onion, vinegar, pepper and melted butter. Fill the fish and sew or skewer the openings.

Cook the fat pork in a flameproof casserole until lightly browned, lay the fish on top, spread with butter and bake in a very moderate oven (350°F. — Gas Mark 3) for about 30 minutes. Add vinegar, tomatoes and sliced onion and continue baking for 10 minutes. Serve very hot.

Bermudan steamed mussels *(Bermuda)*

mussels	lemon or lime juice,
butter	freshly squeezed
salt	bird pepper sherry
pepper	(see page 217)

Put mussels in a pan and cover with salt water. Cover with a closely fitting lid and boil for about 30 minutes, when the water will have boiled away and the mussels opened.

Take out the flesh and put into warmed, individual bowls. With each serving of mussels, serve also a small bowl of melted butter so that each guest can make his own sauce to taste with salt, pepper, lemon juice and bird pepper sherry added to the butter. The mussels are dipped in the sauce as they are eaten.

Boiled fish with sausage meat *(Bahamas)*

6 servings:

2 lb. white fish	2 bay leaves
2 oz. bacon, chopped	1 sprig thyme
1 large onion, chopped	salt
2 potatoes, peeled and diced	1½ pints water
8 oz. sausage meat, diced	juice 2 lemons
small	pinch Cayenne pepper

Leaving the bone in the fish, cut into small steaks and arrange in a saucepan. Add bacon, onion, potatoes, sausage meat, bay leaves, thyme and salt. Pour on water and bring to the boil. Skim, then simmer very gently for 20 minutes. Add lemon juice and pepper just before serving.

Canned salmon mould *(Bahamas)*

4 servings:

2 tablespoons powdered	1½ oz. butter, melted
gelatine	¼ pint milk
¼ pint cold water	2 tablespoons vinegar
2 egg yolks	1 large can red salmon
1 teaspoon salt	2 tablespoons mustard
1 teaspoon mustard	pickle
Cayenne pepper	

Soak gelatine in cold water. Beat egg yolks lightly then beat in salt, mustard, a dash of Cayenne, butter, milk and vinegar. Turn into a double boiler and cook, stirring all the time, until sauce thickens. Then stir in soaked gelatine. Drain salmon, skin and bone it and mix with mustard pickle. Stir into the sauce. Pour into a wetted mould and chill. Turn out and serve with salad.

Crab backs *(British Guiana)*

6 servings: (2 crabs each)

12 small live crabs*	1 tablespoon
1 onion, chopped	Worcestershire sauce or
2–3 teaspoons chives,	vinegar
chopped	salt
2 oz. butter	pepper
	breadcrumbs

* cooked crabs may be used

Place crabs in a large pan, pour on boiling water to cover. Throw this water away, wash crabs, then boil for 30 minutes. Remove claws, break open, pick out the meat, then remove body from shell, keep the eggs and fat and discard the gall. Scrub shells. Brown onion and chives in butter. Add flaked crab meat, Worcestershire sauce, salt and pepper. Refill 8 shells with the mixture, sprinkle with breadcrumbs and brown in a moderately hot oven (400°F. — Gas Mark 5)

* If you are by the sea and able to catch your own crabs, trap them alive and keep them in a safe place for about a week. This is because they eat foul things and should have clean food before being cooked. Give them grass and bread and, if you are in the tropics, add pepper leaves which act as a purge. Plunge crabs into fast boiling water which kills them instantaneously. Break off the legs as soon as they are dead. Then remove the body from the shell and throw away the little black sac or gall.

Note:

On some islands, lime juice is used instead of sauce or vinegar and lard instead of butter.

Crab Creole *(Guadeloupe)*

4 servings:

4 small crabs	Cayenne pepper
¼ lb. breadcrumbs	salt
2 red pepper, chopped finely	dash sherry
	lime or lemon juice
chervil, chopped	clove garlic, crushed
mace, pinch	

Remove flesh from shells and put crab meat in a basin. Mash with a fork, adding enough breadcrumbs to make a paste. Add the peppers, herbs, salt, sherry, juice and garlic, beating in all ingredients.
Scrub the empty shells, and fill with the mixture. Sprinkle with remaining breadcrumbs, dot with butter and bake in a moderate oven (350°F. — Gas Mark 3) till well browned

Crab gumbo *(Barbados)*

4 servings:

2 eggs, hard-boiled	4 tablespoons thin cream
1 oz. butter, melted	8 oz. crab meat
1 oz. flour	salt
juice and finely grated rind of 1 lemon	pepper
2 pints milk	2 tablespoons sherry
	dash Angostura bitters

Mash eggs to a paste and stir into butter. Sift flour, add lemon juice and rind. Bring milk just to the boil and gradually stir into egg mixture, making sure it is smooth. Return to heat and bring to the boil, stirring. Simmer very gently for 5–6 minutes. Remove from heat and briskly stir in the cream. Add flaked crab meat, salt and pepper to taste, sherry and bitters, heat through without boiling and serve hot.

Crab with peppery stuffing *(Jamaica)*

6 servings:

6 crabs, boiled	2 tablespoons butter,
moist breadcrumbs	melted
¼ pint milk	olive oil
4 dashes Tabasco	juice of 1 lemon
3 dashes Angostura bitters	3 tablespoons dry
1 clove of garlic, crushed	breadcrumbs
1 tablespoon chives,	butter
or shallots, chopped	pepper
1½ tablespoons lean bacon,	
minced or finely chopped	

Pick all meat from crab backs and claws. Wash the backs. Flake crab meat and mix with moist breadcrumbs, using 1 part breadcrumbs to 2 parts crab. Moisten mixture with milk mixed with Tabasco and bitters. Fry garlic, chives and bacon in butter until tender. Mix into crab mixture, blending well. Paint shells with olive oil and stuff with mixture. Squeeze lemon juice into each shell, cover with dry breadcrumbs and dot with butter. Bake in a moderate oven (375° F. — Gas Mark 4) until nicely brown. Serve sprinkled with plenty of freshly ground pepper.

Crab soufflé, Paradise Island style *(Bahamas)*

4 servings:

1½ oz. butter	pinch grated nutmeg
1 tablespoon flour	2 eggs, separated
¼ pint milk	2 tablespoons sherry
½ teaspoon salt	1 lb. crab meat, shredded
pinch Cayenne	browned breadcrumbs

Melt the butter, stir in flour and cook, stirring, for 2 minutes. Remove from heat and gradually stir in milk, salt, Cayenne and nutmeg. Return to heat and cook, stirring, until thick.

Continue cooking very gently for 5 minutes. Allow to cool. Lightly beat egg yolks and stir into cooled mixture, then the sherry. Fold in crab, fold in stiffly beaten egg whites and turn into a straight-sided dish, sprinkle with breadcrumbs and stand in a pan of hot water. Bake in a very moderate oven (350° F. — Gas Mark 3) for 45 minutes.

Desert Island fish

4–6 servings:

2 lb. fresh fish	salt
(or frozen fish defrosted)	pepper
fresh lime or lemon juice	

Flake the fish and remove bones. Put in a deep dish and steep in juice for 10 hours. Drain and serve, seasoning to taste.

This is a basic method of serving fish which can be varied according to supplies on your desert island but make sure you are shipwrecked on one where limes or lemons grow. Lemon juice removes strong smells and tenderises the fish tissues by the 'cooking' action of citric acid. I learnt about this at London Airport while waiting for the worst fog in memory to lift. I waited four days with people from all over the world and a lady from Mexico gave me this information. The method was endorsed by the head chef in the B. O. A. C. kitchens who showed me how some of the silver foil dishes of fish that he sends all over the world are cooked by this method en route.

This citric acid tenderising can also be used before cooking fish; the longer it is marinated, the shorter the cooking time. The above recipe becomes slightly more sophisticated if served with raw sliced onion and French dressing (see page 34).

Devilled crawfish, Cat Cay style *(Bahamas)*

4 servings:

4 medium crawfish, boiled	2 tablespoons peanuts,
4 tablespoons butter	chopped
1 tablespoon mustard	2 tomatoes, skinned and
1 teaspoon Worcestershire	chopped
sauce	fingers of new bread
2 bay leaves	2 tablespoons sherry
juice of 2 limes or lemons	1 clove garlic
4 tablespoons mango	grated cheese
chutney (see page 221)	

Split the crawfish and remove all the meat. Cut meat into
$\frac{1}{2}$-inch cubes and wash the shells. Melt butter, add mustard,
sauce, bay leaves, lime or lemon juice, mango chutney,
peanuts, tomatoes and crawfish. Cover closely and cook very
gently for 10–15 minutes. Add a few fingers of new bread and
sherry. Rub shells with cut clove of garlic, stuff with mixture
and sprinkle with grated cheese. Brown under a hot grill.

Escovitch fish *(Jamaica)*

4 servings:

4 green peppers,	1 tablespoon olive oil
cut into eighths	$\frac{1}{4}$ pint vinegar
6 small onions, sliced	2 teaspoons salt
4 carrots, sliced	$\frac{3}{4}$ pint water
3 bay leaves, chopped	2 lb. white fish fillets

Mix peppers, onion, carrots, bay leaves, peppers, olive oil,
vinegar, salt and water in a saucepan, blend well. Bring to the
boil and simmer for 25 minutes. Grill the fish, pour the hot
sauce over it.

In Jamaica, this is almost a National dish. I was shown how
to make it at one of the little houses at Port Royal occupied
by a policeman's family. Port Royal, just near Kingston and

Palisadoes Airport, is now the police headquarters and training centre. It was once Nelson's dockyard and today, tourists can still see his blockhouse and the remains of the defences.

Very near to Port Royal is Morgan's Harbour Beach Club where everyone goes to swim and sunbathe. It was here that the film of the late Ian Fleming's book Dr. No was made and the jetty with small craft moored alongside is familiar to filmgoers.

Fish in coconut milk *(Trinidad)*

4–6 servings:

2 lb. fish, filleted	½ pint coconut cream
3 oz. butter	(see page 42)
	1½ teaspoons salt

Cut fish into convenient sized pieces (flying fish, mullet, sole or any white fish can be used). Heat butter in a frying pan, sauté fish until golden brown on both sides. Add coconut cream and salt, bring to the boil and cook a further 2 minutes.

Fish cutlets *(South Caicos)*

4 servings:

1 lb. fish	breadcrumbs
1 lime or lemon	salt
3 oz. margarine or butter	pepper
	1 egg, lightly beaten

Sprinkle fish with the freshly squeezed lime juice and leave to stand for about 1 hour. Cut into slices, remove central bones and dry. Heat margarine or butter, season breadcrumbs with salt and pepper. Dip fish into egg and then into breadcrumbs. Fry until golden brown.

Fish fritters, Exuma style *(Bahamas)*

4 servings:

1 small can lobster or crab, or fresh lobster or crab	
1 onion chopped	2 oz. butter
1 tomato, chopped and skinned	4 teaspoons baking powder
8 oz. flour	salt
2 eggs, beaten	black pepper
1 green pepper, chopped (optional)	½ pint water
	deep fat for frying

Mix all ingredients except fish and fat, with water to make a batter. Fry fish in deep fat in chunks of convenient size.

Fish fritters are a Bahamian speciality, usually made with conch rather than the more elusive lobster or crab. Just outside sleepy little Georgetown, capital of Great Exuma, is a little bar in a native hut, the door screened with palm fronds nailed together.

Behind the screen, Mrs. Doris Rolle initiated me into the art of fritter making in the true Bahamian way. She is the mother of seven and for eight years has made a living selling conch fritters to fishermen, tourists and passers-by. She is up by 3 a. m. preparing food for the fishermen who bring in her supply of conchs and by 6 a. m. she is busy making fritters, using as many as 50 conchs in a day at Regatta time. Craft from all over the world come to the Out-Island Regatta held each April in the Exumas. This is one of the most beautiful island chains in the Bahamas, getting more popular but still unspoilt.

"Ever'body loves fritters, yes Ma'am," beamed Mrs. Rolle as my lesson finished.

Fish and grape mould *(Haiti)*

6 servings :

2 onions, chopped
4 tablespoons oil
8 tablespoons white
  cooking wine
salt
pepper
1 bay leaf
pinch tumeric
¾ pint water

6 slices carp
2 teaspoons gelatine,
  dissolved in
  1 tablespoon water
6 oz. grapes, peeled,
  halved and seeded
1 custard apple, optional
lemon juice

Sauté onions in oil until soft. Stir in wine, salt, pepper, bay leaf, tumeric and water. Bring to the boil, lower heat and drop in fish slices. Simmer gently for 30 minutes. Remove fish and set aside. Add gelatine to stock and stir in while it is still hot. Remove bay leaf.

Arrange fish in a mould with grapes all round and over it. Pour cooled stock over and leave to set. When firm, turn out and decorate with the custard apple, peeled and quartered, and dipped in lemon juice.

Fish and macaroni pie *(Bermuda)*

4–6 servings:

2 lb. white fish	*For the sauce:*
12 oz. macaroni	2 oz. butter
salt	2 oz. flour
pepper	½ pint milk
2 hard-boiled eggs	breadcrumbs

Simmer fish until just tender in a little water. Drain and reserve liquid for the sauce. Skin, bone and flake the fish. Boil macaroni in salted water until tender and drain. Put a layer of macaroni in a buttered casserole, then a layer of fish, sprinkled with salt and pepper. Continue adding layers of macaroni and fish, with chopped eggs in the middle.

Make the sauce by melting the butter, stirring in the flour and cooking, stirring, for 2 minutes. Remove from heat and gradually stir in milk, and ½ pint fish stock. Bring to the boil, stirring, and cook gently for 5 minutes. Pour over the fish and macaroni, sprinkle with breadcrumbs and bake in a very moderate oven (350° F. — Gas Mark 3) until heated through and browned on top.

St. Croix fish pudding *(U. S. Virgin Islands)*

6 servings:

1 lb. fish, cooked, skinned and boned	2 tablespoons lemon or fresh lime juice
1 1-lb. can salmon, drained	½ teaspoon salt
3 oz. dry breadcrumbs	pinch pepper
2 oz. butter, melted	4 eggs, separated

Flake fish and salmon and mix together with breadcrumbs, butter, lemon juice, salt and pepper. Beat egg yolks until thick and stir into fish mixture. Beat egg whites until very stiff and fold into mixture. Turn into a large greased casserole and bake in a very moderate oven (350° F. — Gas Mark 3) for 30–35 minutes.

Fried Bajan flying fish *(Barbados)*

4 servings:

4 flying fish, boned*   lemon or lime juice

For the batter:

2 tablespoons flour   2 eggs
½ teaspoon salt   ¼ pint water
pepper

oil for frying
lemon or lime, cut into
   wedges

*or herrings

Wash fish in water to which lemon or lime juice has been added. Make a batter (see below), coat the fish then dip in breadcrumbs. Fry till golden brown, drain and serve with lemon or lime wedges.
To make the batter: Mix flour, salt and pepper, add the eggs and enough water to make a smooth creamy paste which covers the back of a spoon easily. Beat until very smooth, then coat the fish.
To fry, use a deep wire basket and have the oil smoking hot (blue smoke) but not actually burning.

'Bajan' means Barbadian and it was at one of the loveliest places on the island that I learnt how to cook flying fish. This was at Sam Lord's Castle, a Regency house built by a buck, far from his native Brighton, which is now an hotel. Sam Lord became more buccaneer than buck once his castellated house was complete with huge cellars, mirrored walls, brass-bound furniture and a huge shower, fit for six men, which still stands in the garden on the way down to the beach. There is still his turtle tank by the sea and although today there are air-conditioned annex rooms, there is a feeling of past Regency splendour right through the castle.

Fresh fish pie *(Bahamas)*

6 servings:

2½ lb. fish	1 egg, lightly beaten
2 oz. butter	8 oz. cheese, grated
2 oz. flour	salt
½ pint milk	2 tablespoons sherry

Wash fish and cook until just tender in boiling salted water. Drain and reserve stock. Skin, bone and flake the fish. Melt butter, stir in flour and cook, stirring, for 2 minutes. Remove from heat and gradually stir in milk and ½ pint fish liquid. Add egg and most of the cheese, with salt to taste. Stir thoroughly and return to heat and cook, stirring, until thick. Stir in sherry and gently fold in flaked fish. Turn into a buttered casserole, sprinkle with remaining cheese and bake in a very moderate oven (350° F. — Gas Mark 3) for about 20 minutes, when the top should be nicely brown.

Island stuffed crawfish *(Turks Island)*

4–6 servings:

1 large crawfish or lobster	2 slices of green pepper
1 large onion, diced	salt
2 sticks celery, finely chopped	black pepper
2 teaspoons fresh parsley, chopped	2 oz. butter
	4 oz. browned breadcrumbs
	paprika

Boil crawfish by plunging into rapidly boiling salted water and boil until the shell turns bright red, about 15 minutes. Take out and put in cold water immediately. Split and remove the flesh. Wash the shell. Shred the crawfish meat.

Mix onion, celery, parsley, green pepper and salt and black pepper to taste. Fry gently in butter until soft. Stir in breadcrumbs and crawfish and continue cooking until lightly brown, stirring occasionally. Pack into crawfish shell, sprinkle with paprika and bake in a moderately hot oven (400° F. — Gas Mark 5) for 20 minutes. Serve immediately, in the shell.

Lobster casserole *(Bermuda)*

4–6 servings:

1 medium mild onion, chopped fine	$\frac{1}{4}$ teaspoon curry powder
1 green pepper, chopped	$\frac{1}{4}$ teaspoon chilli powder
4 oz. mushrooms, sliced	$\frac{1}{4}$ teaspoon mustard
2 oz. butter	fine breadcrumbs, dried
8–12. oz. lobster meat, cooked	grated cheese
	salt
$\frac{1}{4}$ pint cream sauce (see page 31)	pepper
	extra butter

Fry onion, pepper and mushrooms in butter for 5 minutes. Turn into a buttered casserole and cover with lobster. Heat cream sauce and stir in the seasonings. Pour over lobster, sprinkle well with breadcrumbs and cheese. Add a little seasoning, dot with butter and grill lightly for 10–15 minutes.

Lobster catablanc, Montagu Beach style *(Bahamas)*

4 servings:

2 cloves garlic, finely chopped	2 tomatoes, chopped
1 small onion, finely chopped	2 1-lb. lobsters, boiled
2 tablespoons olive oil	1 tablespoon flour
1 bay leaf	6 tablespoons red wine
2 pimentos, chopped	6 tablespoons water
	juice $\frac{1}{2}$ lemon
	salt and pepper

Fry garlic and onion in oil until golden brown. Add bay leaf, pimentos, tomatoes and lobster meat cut in 1-inch dice. Cook gently for 10 minutes. Stir in flour then add remaining ingredients. Simmer for 15 minutes and serve with boiled rice.

Lobster Creole *(Puerto Rico)*

6 servings:

2 onions, chopped
2 large green peppers, chopped
2 cloves garlic, crushed
4 tablespoons olive oil
1½ teaspoons salt
pinch pepper
2 large tomatoes, peeled, cored and quartered
2 8-oz. cans tomato sauce
2 lb. lobster meat, cooked and shredded
4 tablespoons white wine
boiled rice
pickled red peppers

Sauté onions, peppers and garlic in olive oil until tender but not browned. Stir in salt and pepper. Add tomato quarters and cook gently until tender. Stir in tomato sauce, and lobster. Simmer for 15 minutes. Stir in wine and cook for 3 minutes. Serve with rice and decorate with peppers.

Note:

If the lobster is omitted, this recipe makes a splendid sauce or dip for any shell fish or white fish dish. The Lobster Creole can be made with any boiled lobster, including lobster tails, or canned lobster may be substituted.

Lobster curry, Gorda style *(British Virgin Islands)*

6 servings:

3 small lobsters
2 tablespoons olive oil
6 oz. butter
1 mild onion, finely chopped
1 green pepper, finely chopped
1 apple, finely chopped
1 tablespoon coconut, grated
3 tablespoons white wine
3 tablespoons curry powder
1 teaspoon tumeric powder
2 tablespoons tomato paste
stock
salt
½ pint thick white sauce (see page 41)
1 tablespoon chutney

Cut the tails from the lobsters and divide each lobster into 6. Fry it in oil and butter until light brown. Add onion, pepper, apple, coconut and wine and cook for a further 5 minutes. Transfer to a casserole and stir in curry powder, tumeric, tomato paste and stock to cover. Season to taste and bake in a very moderate oven (350° F. — Gas Mark 3) for 30 minutes. Take out the lobster pieces and extract meat from the tails. Set aside. Reduce sauce by half, thicken with white sauce and stir in chutney. Season to taste, add lobster meat, coat thoroughly then heat through in the oven. Serve with hot boiled rice.

Lobster Newburg *(Antigua)*

6–8 servings:

4 oz. butter	4 egg yolks
4 lb. lobster,	½ pint cream
boiled and picked	2 tablespoons brandy
2 teaspoons salt	2 tablespoons sherry
dash Cayenne pepper	toast
pinch grated nutmeg	

Melt the butter and fry lobster very gently in it for 5 minutes. Stir in salt, pepper and nutmeg. Beat egg yolks, beat in cream, then stir into the lobster. Cook gently, stirring with a wooden spoon, until mixture thickens. Add sherry and brandy and serve on toast.

Melba toast

Cut very thin slices of bread, spread them on a baking sheet, place in a hot oven, 400° F., — Gas Mark 7 for 10 minutes. This toast can be stored in a tin when cold.

Lobster rissoles *(St. Kitts)*

2–4 servings:

1 lobster, boiled and picked	3 tablespoons flour
2 egg yolks, hard-boiled	3 eggs
pinch Cayenne	¼ pint milk
salt	butter for frying

Mince lobster or chop it finely. Mix with crumbled egg yolks and Cayenne and salt to taste. Sift flour, drop in eggs and beat. Beat in milk, using only enough to make a stiff batter. Mix in lobster to make a stiff paste. Roll into balls and fry in butter.

Lobster risotto *(St. Lucia)*

4 servings:

1 large onion	2 bay leaves
2 cloves garlic	pinch saffron
4 oz. butter	salt
1 lobster, boiled	pepper
4 oz. chicken liver	12 oz. rice
2 oz. mushrooms	1½ pints stock
1 pimento	grated cheese
6 anchovies	tomato sherry sauce (see page 41)

Chop onion and garlic finely and fry in an ovenproof dish in butter until lightly browned. Add diced lobster and chopped liver, mushrooms, pimento and anchovies. Stir in bay leaves, saffron, salt, pepper, rice and stock. Bring to the boil, cover tightly and cook in a moderately hot oven (400°F. — Gas Mark 5) for 20 minutes. Serve with grated cheese and tomato sherry sauce.

Lobster Sal Cay *(Bahamas)*

2–4 servings:

1 medium lobster	2 egg yolks
2 oz. butter	4 tablespoons thin cream
1 small onion, finely	salt
chopped	hot buttered toast
4 green olives, stoned	paprika
2–3 tablespoons brandy	

Boil lobster in salted water for 20 minutes. Allow to cool and remove flesh. Cut into 1-inch dice. Melt butter without browning it, stir in onion, olives, lobster and brandy. Simmer for 2 minutes. Beat yolks and cream and pour into the pan. Heat through very gently but do not boil. Season with salt and serve on toast with a sprinkling of paprika.

Lobster stew, Chef Anthony Style *(Bahamas)*

4 servings:

1 large lobster	¼ pint thin cream
6 oz. butter	paprika
salt	8 toasted biscuits or
pepper	Melba toast (see page 105)

Halve the lobster down the back. Dot with most of the butter and season with salt and pepper. Place in a baking tin and put into a hot oven (400°F. — Gas Mark 5). When the juices begin to flow from the lobtster and the flesh becomes tender, remove from oven and pick meat from the shell and claws. Put the juice in a saucepan and add the finely chopped lobster meat. Stir in cream and bring to the boil. Remove from heat, stir in remaining butter and sprinkle with paprika. Serve on biscuits or Melba toast.

Lobster stuffed (Bermuda)

8 servings:

4 lobsters, boiled
1 lb. scallops
4 tablespoons white wine
2 tablespoons sherry
4 tablespoons water
1 bay leaf
salt, Cayenne pepper
few peppercorns
3-4 tablespoons sour
    cream

fresh dill or parsley,
    chopped
For the sauce:
4 oz. butter
4 oz. flour
3 tablespoons thin cream
1 egg yolk
2 oz. mushrooms,
    finely sliced
grated cheese

Split lobsters and take meat out. Wash shells thoroughly and set aside. Clean scallops and put into a saucepan with wine, sherry, water, bay leaf, salt and peppercorns. Bring slowly to the boil, cook for 2 minutes, then strain. Set aside the liquid for the sauce. Chop scallops and lobster meat and mix together with sour cream and a little dill or parsley. Season with salt and pepper and fill lobster shells with the mixture.
To make the sauce: Melt 2½ oz. butter. Stir in flour sifted with seasoning. Cook, stirring, for 2 minutes. Remove from heat and gradually stir in scallop stock. Return to heat and stir until sauce comes to the boil. Add ½ oz. butter, a little at a time. Beat cream with yolk and stir in, add mushrooms. Pour sauce over lobster, dot with remaining butter, sprinkle with cheese and brown under grill.

Lobster Thermidor (Bermuda)

4 servings:

2 medium lobsters,
    boiled
2 oz. butter
4 oz. mushrooms, cooked
1 teaspoon paprika
2 tablespoons sherry

¾ pint cream sauce
    (see page 31)
2 dashes Tabasco sauce
½ teaspoon salt
pepper
grated cheese

Split the lobsters and remove meat. Wash shells well and set aside. Cut meat into 1-inch dice. Melt butter, add lobster and chopped mushrooms. Sprinkle with paprika and cook gently for 2 minutes, shaking the pan. Pour sherry over and simmer until it is reduced by half. Stir in cream sauce, Tabasco, salt and pepper. Boil for 1 minute. Turn mixture into shells, sprinkle with plenty of grated cheese and brown under the grill.

Miss Lou's simmering salt fish and achee
(Jamaica)

4 servings:

1 lb. salt fish	4 oz. butter or margarine
(see page 112)	3 tablespoons tomato
12 achees, boiled	pureé
2 oz. salt pork or bacon,	$\frac{1}{8}$ teaspoon black pepper
fried	

Cook fish in boiling water until done. Skin, bone and flake it, then mix with achees and pork or bacon. Melt butter, stir in the tomato pureé and season with black pepper. Pour over the fish mixture and bake in a moderate oven, (375° F. — Gas Mark 4) until it starts to simmer. Serve at once.

Salt fish and achee is another of the 'Jamaica coat of arms' dishes. So I asked Louise Bennett to tell me how to make it. Louise, or 'Miss Lou' as she is known all through the island, is a sort of Jamaican Gracie Fields, a national idol as well as an authority on folklore and dialect. She is on radio and in the annual pantomime at Kingston's Ward theatre which is a once-in-a-year outing for half the population; it was she who wrote and recited the verse for Princess Margaret at Independence celebrations. She observes the Jamaican character with humorous and humanitarian skill. I spent a fascinating day at her home in Gordon Town where she is squire to the district. As we drove through the village, people crowded round her little car calling "Hi, Miss Lou, safe journey, Miss Lou."

Old wife (*Jamaica*)

old wife fish or sole   breadcrumbs
  (one per serving)   butter
flour   parsley
1 egg, lightly beaten

Wash fish carefully and dry well. Dust over a little flour, dip into egg, then breadcrumbs and fry a light brown in butter. Serve with melted butter, garnish with parsley.

Oven fried scallops (*Bermuda*)

4 servings:

1 lb. scallops   dried breadcrumbs
2 tablespoons salad oil   salt
2 tablespoons lemon juice   pepper
  or fresh lime juice   paprika
1 egg, lightly beaten   2 oz. butter
2 tablespoons water   1 lemon or lime

Clean scallops and marinate for at least 1 hour in oil and lemon or lime juice beaten together. Stir occasionally. Drain scallops and dip in mixed egg and water. Roll in breadcrumbs seasoned with salt, pepper and paprika. Arrange scallops in a shallow baking dish, pour melted butter over. Bake in a hot oven (450° F. — Gas Mark 7) for 15–20 minutes when they should be brown and crisp on the outside. Serve with lemon wedges.

Pimentade of shellfish (*Bimini*)

4 servings:

2 lobsters or 2–4 crabs   2 small onions, chopped
4 tablespoons lemon   stick celery, chopped
  or lime juice   dash Tabasco
pinch basil, thyme and   2 tablespoons dry white
  rosemary, chopped   wine
½ clove garlic   ½ pint water
½ bay leaf   quarters of lemon or lime

Marinate shell fish in lemon or lime juice for at least 4 hours. Meanwhile, cover head and tail trimmings with cold water, add sweet herbs, garlic, bay leaf, onions and celery and bring to the boil. Simmer for 15 minutes and strain. Into this stock drop the chillies and marinated fish, together with liquid in which it soaked and the Tabasco. Poach gently until tender. Remove fish and keep warm. Make a sauce by reducing ½ pint stock with white wine. Pour over fish and serve with lemons.

Poached rock fish with egg sauce (Bermuda)

6 servings:

6 slices rock fish or any large white fish	water
	4 sticks celery
fresh lime or lemon juice	sprig parsley
salt	1 onion, sliced
pepper	3 cloves

For the sauce:

1 oz. butter	½ teaspoon
1 oz. flour	Worcestershire sauce
½ pint milk	salt
1 egg, beaten	pepper
pinch mustard	2 tablespoons chopped parsley

Wash fish, squeeze juice over it and sprinkle with salt and pepper. Stand at room temperature for 1 hour. Drain and arrange in a large frying pan. Add just enough water to cover, stir in chopped celery, parsley, onion and cloves and poach gently for 30 minutes.

Make the sauce: melt butter, stir in flour and cook for a few minutes, stirring. Stir in milk gradually, bring to the boil, stirring, and simmer for 5 minutes. Allow to cool a little before beating in egg, mustard, sauce, salt and pepper. Cook, stirring, until thick and smooth. Add parsley and pour over fish just before serving.

Salt fish in chemise *(Dominica)*

4 servings

1 lb. salt fish (seasoned smoked or fresh fish, can be substituted)	1 small onion, chopped
	1 tomato, chopped
	1 tablespoon flour
3 tablespoons oil or butter	¾ pint water
¼ teaspoon pepper	pinch thyme
2 chives	4 eggs

Scald fish, skin and bone it and flake finely. Heat oil or butter and lightly fry onion, tomato, chives and thyme. Stir in flour, then water. Add fish and simmer for 10 minutes. Turn into a greased casserole and break eggs over the mixture. Season and steam, covered, until eggs are set.

Note:

This dish can be made in individual fire-proof dishes, using 1 egg to each and ¼ lb. fish per person. If fresh fish is used, add a pinch of salt to each serving.

To salt fish:

Salmon or cod are both good for salting; mackerel is a good choice of smaller fish or, in the tropics, use king fish.

Remove the head and bone the fish by cutting down the back and separating flesh from backbone. Keep the flesh in one large piece while removing bone and entrails. Wipe fish with a wet cloth but do not wash. With a sharp knife, make slashes from head to tail on the inside. Rub all over with salt working it in well. About 10 tablespoons is necessary as a rule, but more may be used if required.

Put fish on a flat dish and leave for 1 day. Pour off the brine solution which results, wipe the fish again with a clean cloth and allow to dry for several days. In the tropics, the drying is done in the sun, but a warm place near the boiler is also suitable.

Salmon loaf *(Bahamas)*

4 servings:

1 can salmon	4 oz. butter, melted
4 eggs	3 oz. breadcrumbs

Mash salmon, beat in eggs and butter and stir in breadcrumbs. Turn into a buttered basin or mould and steam for 1 hour. Serve hot or cold.

Sambel goreng oedang *(Surinam)*

6 servings:

4 tablespoons onion, finely chopped	1 teaspoon lemon or lime juice
1 clove garlic	pinch salt
2 tablespoons olive oil	8 oz. shrimps, shelled and cut into small pieces
pepper to taste	
½ teaspoon brown sugar, the dark variety if possible	2 bay leaves
	½ pint coconut cream (see page 31)

Sauté the onion and garlic in the olive oil; add the pepper, sugar, juice and salt, blend well. Add shrimps, coconut cream and bay leaves and cook gently for 25 minutes, or until the shrimps are tender. Remove bay leaves before serving.

This is part of the 'very small rice table', or modified 'Rijsttafel', the East Indian rice dinner. Rice should be served in a separate bowl and, according to East Indian cooking procedure, the merest pinch of salt is enough. Many of the rice table dishes are highly spiced and very hot, but this one is mild and makes a pleasant first course. The quantities given are intended only for an appetiser, not a main dish.

Shrimp curry *(British Guiana)*

4 servings:

3 oz. butter
1 onion, chopped
½ clove garlic,
 finely sliced
2 tablespoons curry powder
⅓ pint water or coconut
 cream (see page 31)

green mango, tamarind,
 lime or lemon juice
salt
1 lb. shrimps
boiled rice

Heat butter and fry onion and garlic gently in it without browning. Stir in curry powder and cook, stirring, for 3 minutes. Stir in water or coconut milk with mango, tamarind, lime or lemon juice and salt to taste. Cook gently until thickened. Put in shrimps and cook gently until tender, shaking the pan occasionally to prevent sticking. Do not stir after adding shrimps. Serve with rice.

Smothered grouper *(Bahamas)*

6 servings:

2 lb. grouper fillets
scant ¼ pint water
2 tablespoons lemon or
 lime juice
1 tablespoon vinegar
black pepper
ground chilli pepper
 (optional)

1 egg
4 oz. breadcrumbs
2 small onions,
 finely sliced
1½ oz. butter
1 can tomatoes, drained
salt
pepper

Wash fillets and score slightly. Mix 4 tablespoons water, lemon or lime juice and vinegar. Pour over fillets and allow to stand for 4 minutes. Drain and wipe fish with a clean, dry cloth. Sprinkle all over with black and chilli pepper. Beat egg lightly with remaining water. Dip fillets first in egg and then in breadcrumbs and fry for 6–7 minutes each side until golden brown. Meanwhile, sauté onions in butter until tender, stir in chopped tomatoes, salt and pepper to taste. Simmer for 5 minutes, stirring occasionally. Add fish to onion and tomato mixture and simmer for 5 minutes. Serve fish covered with sauce.

Note:
Grouper is rather like sea bass, but halibut or cod fillets may be substituted.

Snapper savoury *(Jamaica*

4 servings:

1 lb. snapper fillets	salt
2 teaspoons fresh lime or lemon juice	pepper

For the sauce:

2 oz. butter	4 oz. cheese, grated
1 oz. flour	butter
½ pint milk	seasoning
toast	onion salt

Arrange fillets in a casserole, sprinkle with lime or lemon juice and a little salt and pepper. Leave to stand.
Make the sauce: melt butter, stir in flour and cook, stirring for 1 minute. Remove from heat and gradually stir in milk. Add most of the cheese, season and bring to the boil, stirring. Reduce heat and cook gently for 5 minutes. Pour over fillets, sprinkle with remaining cheese and dot with butter. Bake in a very moderate oven (350° F. — Gas Mark 3), for about 20 minutes, until browned. Serve with quarters of toast sprinkled with onion salt.

Note:
Any firm, white-fleshed fish may be used.

Steamed Bajan flying-fish *(Barbados)*

4 servings:

4 flying fish*	salt
2 onions, sliced	pepper
2 tomatoes, sliced	1 tablespoon butter,
1 tablespoon lemon	melted
or fresh lime juice	

* Herring or whiting may be substituted

Clean and bone fish carefully. Season well with salt and pepper, then fold each fish over, putting the tail through the mouth. Arrange in a dish, add a little boiling water, top with onion and tomato slices. Sprinkle with lime or lemon juice, season, then pour over the butter. Cover closely and steam until fish is tender.

Tuna and crawfish soufflé *(New Providence)*

4–6 servings:

2 tablespoons butter	1 teaspoon curry
4 tablespoons flour	powder (optional)
½ pint milk	4 eggs, separated
½ pint fish stock	salt
1 tablespoon parsley,	pepper
freshly chopped	paprika
1 onion, chopped fine	8 oz. tuna, cooked and
2 tablespoons lime juice,	shredded
or lemon juice	8 oz. crawfish, cooked
4 oz. dried breadcrumbs	and shredded

Melt butter, stir in flour and cook, stirring for a minute. Gradually stir in milk, then fish stock and bring to the boil, stirring. Cook for about 5 minutes until very thick. Add parsley, onion, lime or lemon juice, breadcrumbs and curry powder. Beat egg yolks and stir in, then the fish, and salt, pepper and paprika to taste. Whisk egg whites until very stiff and fold into mixture. Put into a greased casserole or ring mould and bake in a very moderate oven (350° F. — Gas Mark 3) for 25–30 minutes. Serve hot or cold.

Turtle pot pie, Montagu Beach style *(Bahamas)*

4–6 servings

2 lb. green turtle meat, (callipee)	pinch thyme
	pinch rosemary
4 oz. butter	pinch marjoram
1 large onion, chopped	1 4-oz. tomato purée
1 clove garlic, chopped	1 egg
1 carrot, diced	salt
1 potato, diced	pinch cinnamon
4 oz. breadcrumbs	pepper
1 tablespoon flour	2 pints water
2 bay leaves	4 oz. pastry (see page 118)

Cut half the turtle meat into 1-inch cubes. Fry onion and garlic in butter till golden brown. Add cubed turtle and 1 tablespoon flour and mix. Add tomato pureé, carrot, potato and herbs; pour water over and simmer for 30 minutes.

Mince remaining turtle meat, mix with breadcrumbs, egg and cinnamon and form into small balls. Drop these in stew and allow to boil for 5 minutes after stew is cooked. Put stew into a deep pie dish, cover with pastry lid and cook in a moderate oven (350° F. — Gas Mark 3) until golden brown.

Note:

The islands still abound with turtle in some parts, although in others it is becoming more of a rarity each year. Yet however difficult, it can be obtained in most parts of the world, and no Caribbean cookery book would be complete without turtle recipes. To most of us it is a delicacy, but on one island I visited, turtle steak was fed to animals.

The green turtle meat, from the body, is called callipee and the yellow meat taken from the fins is known as callipash. Pork or veal can be substituted in all turtle recipes.

Pastry, flaky

4 oz. plain flour	3 oz. butter or margarine
pinch salt	3–4 tablespoons cold water

Sieve the flour and salt into a mixing bowl. Divide the butter or margarine into four. Rub one portion into the flour. Place remainder in a cool place until required. Mix in the water to a fairly soft dough with the blade of a knife. Turn out on a lightly-floured board. Knead for about 5 minutes until it is smooth and silky. Sprinkle with flour; cover with a damp cloth or polythene bag and leave to rest for about 15 minutes. Roll out to an oblong approximately 5 inches by $2\frac{1}{2}$ inches. Brush off any surplus flour. Dab the second portion of butter or margarine in rows over the top two-thirds of the dough leaving a margin of half an inch round the edge. Fold the uncovered third upwards and the top third downwards and over to cover it. Lightly press the three open edges with the rolling-pin to seal. Turn the dough round so that the right-hand edge faces you. Lightly roll out to an oblong approximately $4\frac{1}{2}$ inches by 3 inches. Brush off any surplus flour. Dab the third portion of butter or margarine over as for second portion. Fold and seal the edges as before. Place on a floured plate; sprinkle with flour; cover with a damp cloth or polythene bag. Rest in a cold place for 20 minutes.

Repeat the rolling process, using the last portion of butter or margarine, but it is not necessary at this stage to rest the dough. Repeat the rolling process again, without adding any more butter or margarine. Rest as before.

After the last rolling and resting, the pastry is ready to roll to the thickness stated in the recipe used.

Note:

In hot weather, rest dough after *every* folding and sealing and if the dough is very sticky or patchy, give an extra folding and rolling.

Turtle steak No. 1 (*Jamaica*)

4–6 servings:

2 lb. turtle steak
lime juice or lemon juice
4 oz. lard
black pepper
2 onions, sliced finely

2 tomatoes, sliced finely
butter
flour
lime or lemon slices

Rub steak well with lime juice. Make lard very hot and put steak in whole. Sprinkle with black pepper, add onion and tomato. Cover and cook gently for 10–15 minutes. By then it should have made its own juice but if there is not enough, add a little water. Continue cooking until steak is done, a further 10–15 minutes. If a thick gravy is preferred, stir together a little melted butter and a little flour. Mix to a smooth paste with some of the steak gravy and stir into the pan. Cook, stirring until thickened.
Serve with another squeeze of lime or lemon juice and slices of lime or lemon.

Turtle steak No. 2 (*St. Thomas*)

4–6 servings:

2 lb. turtle steak, cut into
  1½ inches by ½ inch strips
2 sticks celery, chopped
1 onion, minced
1 tomato, chopped
3 mushrooms, chopped
1 clove garlic, chopped
1 small can tomato purée

2 sprigs parsley, chopped
½ pint dry white wine
1 tablespoon flour
1 teaspoon salt
pinch sweet basil
pinch thyme
pinch marjoram
dash brandy

Put celery, onion, tomato, mushrooms, garlic, tomato purée and parsley in a pan with wine and blend well. Mix flour, salt and herbs; stir into mixture and bring to the boil, stirring from time to time. Add turtle strips, blend and transfer all to a casserole. Bake for 1¼ hours in a very moderate oven (350° F. — Gas Mark 3). If necessary cook a further 15 minutes. Before removing from oven, stir in brandy.

119

Turtle stew *(Jamaica)*

4 servings:

2 lb. stewing turtle meat	pinch thyme
salt	10 cloves
lime juice or lemon juice	pinch grated nutmeg
2 pints water	pinch pepper
1 stick cinnamon	1–2 tablespoons flour
1 large onion, chopped	2 tablespoons sherry
4 tomatoes, chopped	lime quarters or lemon
small bunch parsley, chopped	quarters

Rub meat well with salt and lime juice and place in cold water. Add cinnamon, onion, tomatoes, parsley, thyme, cloves, nutmeg and pepper. Cook over a very low heat for 3 hours, adding more water if it gets too low. About 15 minutes before serving, mix flour with a little water and stir in to thicken the stew, according to taste. Stir well as it thickens. Just before serving, stir in sherry and serve with lime quarters to squeeze over the meat.

Meats and poultry

Meats are cooked in very varied ways through the many islands of the Caribbean: it is impossible to indicate any one style. Native stews are very simple, like the Montserrat 'goat water'; curried goat is a staple item of diet in Jamaica; in Barbados and British Guiana, pepperpot is an everyday dish.

Barbecue and spit-roasted recipes are very good for all outdoor meals but none are confined to outdoor cooking, as many people have a turning spit in the kitchen.

Creole cooking is for the sophisticated, as are most of the recipes from Haiti, Puerto Rico and those of East Indian origin. There are not many beef dishes, because this meat is not very plentiful. Goat and chicken are most easily found and therefore more recipes for these are included.

Once again, bananas, pineapple, oranges and lemons are used in cooking and garnishing; spices, and rum for flavouring. Paw-paw, or papaya, is a wonderful tenderiser (see page 21).

Alicot *(Jamaica)*

4 servings:

1½ lb. chicken giblets, cooked and allowed to get cold, cooked veal or lean pork	1 teaspoon tomato purée
	sprig thyme
bacon fat or dripping	1 bay leaf
2 onions	½ pint vegetable or meat stock
2 rashers bacon, diced	salt
	pepper

Cut giblets or meat into small pieces, brown lightly in dripping. Remove meat from pan, fry onions and bacon in the same fat, adding tomato purée, thyme and bay leaf. Add meat and stock, season and bring to boil. Simmer gently for 1 hour. Remove thyme and bay leaf and serve with sliced cooked potatoes or yams.

Baked Blue Mountain pigeon *(Jamaica)*

4 servings:

1½ lb. potatoes, boiled and mashed	8 blue mountain pigeons
	8 tablespoons Madeira
4 tablespoons peanuts, roasted and chopped	8 rashers lean bacon, chopped and fried
2 oz. butter	butter for basting

Mix potatoes with peanuts and 1½ oz. butter and stuff prepared birds. Arrange in a baking dish, cover, and bake in a moderate oven (375°F. — Gas Mark 4) for 25–30 minutes, basting frequently with butter. Remove birds to a warmed serving dish and pour over about 6 tablespoons Madeira. Surround birds with bacon, remaining wine and butter to dilute the liquid in the baking pan. Cook and stir until very hot and slightly reduced before serving with the pigeons.

Note:

Cornish game hen can be cooked like this using 1 bird per serving.

122

Baked ham with bananas

4 servings:

2 slices ham, 1-inch thick
2 bananas, peeled and
   sliced
3 oz. brown sugar

4 tablespoons coconut,
   freshly grated
4 tablespoons lime or
   lemon juice
1 oz. butter

Halve ham slices and arrange in a shallow, greased baking dish. Smother with banana, sprinkle with sugar, coconut and lime juice. Dot liberally with butter and bake in a very moderate oven (350°F. — Gas Mark 3) for 25–30 minutes.

Barbecued spareribs *(St. Eustatius)*

4–6 servings:

3 tablespoons soy sauce
3 tablespoons honey
2 tablespoons vinegar
1 tablespoon sherry
2 teaspoons sugar

$\frac{1}{2}$ teaspoon ground ginger
6 tablespoons beef stock
1 clove garlic, crushed
$3\frac{1}{2}$–4 lb. spareribs

Beat together the soy sauce, honey, vinegar, sherry, sugar, ground ginger, stock and garlic, blending thoroughly. Pour over spareribs, left whole, and marinate for 2 hours, turning and basting frequently. Take out the ribs and lay on a rack in a baking tin. Bake in a very moderate oven (350°F. — Gas Mark 3) for 1–$1\frac{1}{4}$ hours, pouring off the fat and basting with marinade frequently. When cooked, cut into individual ribs and serve with any baste which remains.

St. Eustatius is usually known simply as 'Statia'. The chief crop is yams and the local drink is a kind of grog known as 'Miss Blyden'.

Caribbean kebabs *(Anguilla)*

6 servings:

1 lb. rump steak
3 tomatoes,
2 onions
1 green pepper

For basting:

1 tablespoon West India
treacle
4 tablespoons pineapple
juice

1 can pineapple chunks,
drained or fresh
pineapple
2 tablespoons vinegar
2 tablespoons cooking oil
seasoning to taste
cooked rice

Cut steak into 1-inch cubes, quarter tomatoes, peel and cut onions into chunks, seed and cut green pepper into squares. Skewer the meat, vegetables and pineapple alternately on 6 skewers. Lay kebabs in grill pan.

Combine basting ingredients and pour over kebabs. Cook under a hot grill for 10 minutes, turning the skewers frequently and basting often.

Serve on a bed of rice with the remaining basting liquid poured over.

Note:

Alternatively, make the barbecue baste by frying 1 small chopped onion in 2 tablespoons oil. Stir in 2 tablespoons tomato purée, 2 tablespoons West India treacle, 2 tablespoons vinegar, 4 tablespoons water, salt and pepper to taste.

Chicken with almonds *(Trinidad)*

4 servings:

2 tablespoons onion,
  finely chopped
3 tablespoons cucumber,
  chopped
3 tablespoons carrot,
  chopped
1 4-oz. can mushrooms,
  drained

¾ pint boiling water
1 lb. raw chicken meat,
  diced
2 tablespoons olive oil
1 teaspoon salt
4 tablespoons almonds,
  blanched

Turn all vegetables into a bowl and pour water over. Stand for 10 minutes and drain. Meanwhile, sauté chicken in 1 tablespoon oil on a gentle heat for 15 minutes. Add vegetables and stir in salt, mixing all well together. Continue cooking gently for 5 minutes. Sauté almonds separately in the oil and serve chicken with almonds piled on top.

Chicken barbecued *(Tobago)*

4–6 servings:

1 4-lb. roasting chicken
2 cloves garlic, crushed
2 teaspoons salt
pinch pepper

1 teaspoon brown sugar
1½ teaspoons mixed spice
2 tablespoons oil

Clean chicken and dry inside and out. Make a sauce of garlic, salt, pepper, sugar, spice and oil, beating well together. Rub into the bird, outside and in, and allow to stand for at least 1 hour.
Stand chicken on a rack in a roasting pan and roast in the centre of a hot oven (425° F. — Gas Mark 6) for 1½–2 hours, until bird is well browned and tender, basting with marinade and turning frequently.
Carve chicken, chop meat in 1-inch wide strips, Chinese fashion, and serve.

Chicken breast in papers *(Barbados)*

4–5 servings:

breast of 2 chickens
1 tablespoon olive oil
4 oz. mushrooms, minced
2 tablespoons scallions or
shallots, minced

¼ teaspoon ground ginger
pinch cinnamon
3 teaspoons sherry
fat for frying

Skin and bone chicken breasts; lay between sheets of waxed paper and pound till very thin. Remove top and cut chicken into 2-inch squares.

Heat oil, mix mushrooms and scallions, fry in oil for 5 minutes, shaking pan to prevent sticking. Stir in ginger, cinnamon and sherry; allow to cool.

Cut greaseproof paper or foil into 4–5 8-inch squares. Divide chicken meat equally beetwen between them.

Spread cooled mixture in a layer on each heap of chicken pieces. Fold paper to make little envelopes. Heat fat until very hot, drop in envelopes, one or two at a time, fry for 5 minutes each. Drain and serve very hot in the envelopes

Chicken calypso *(Domenica)*

4 servings:

4 quarters frying chicken
4 tablespoons oil
1 lb. rice, well-washed
2 tablespoons onion,
minced
2 tablespoons green pepper,
minced

½ teaspoon saffron
1 pint chicken stock
4 oz. mushrooms, sliced
finely
1 tablespoon rum
1 slice lemon or lime peel
dash Angostura bitters

Sauté chicken in oil until brown all over. Remove chicken, then add rice, onion and pepper. Fry until golden. Stir in saffron, stock, mushrooms, rum and lemon or lime peel. Arrange chicken on top, add bitters and cover closely. Simmer slowly until rice is tender and liquid absorbed. Remove lid for about 5 minutes before cooking is finished, so that rice is light and fluffy.

Chicken in coconut shells *(Jamaica)*

4 servings:

4 small coconuts	1 green pepper, seeded
1 frying chicken, boned,	and chopped
skinned and diced	1 clove garlic, crushed
4 rashers fat bacon,	1 teaspoon brown sugar
chopped	2 dashes Tabasco
salt	1 bay leaf
1 large onion, peeled and	4 teaspoons white wine
finely chopped	

Crack coconuts by puncturing two eyes, draining milk and, with nut, eyes down, on stone or concrete, strike it sharply with a hammer.

Prepare chicken and sweat bacon. Add chicken pieces and pinch salt and fry until brown. Remove the meat.

Fry onion, green pepper and garlic in remaining fat until tender. Stir in sugar, Tabaco, chicken and bacon pieces. Fill coconut shells about two-thirds full, adding $\frac{1}{4}$ bay leaf and 1 teaspoon white wine to each nut.

Tie lids on with string, stand in a pan in 1 inch water and bake in a moderate oven (375°F. — Gas Mark 4) for 45 minutes.

Serve with aubergine, sweet corn or cucumber.

Chicken, jellied *(Grand Bahama)*

4 servings:

1 chicken	salt
water	pepper
1 oz. granulated gelatine	2 eggs, hard-boiled and
1 tablespoon	quartered
Worcestershire sauce	

Cover chicken with cold water and bring to the boil. Simmer gently until tender. Remove chicken, then boil stock rapidly to reduce it to 2 pints. Stir in gelatine, sauce, and salt and pepper to taste, strain and allow to cool but not set.
Meanwhile, remove meat from chicken and shred into neat strips using the fingers rather than a knife. Add chicken and eggs to stock. Turn into a prepared mould and chill until thoroughly set.

Note:

Flavourings, such as bay leaf and other herbs may be added to the chicken as it cooks and removed before reducing the stock.

Chicken the Liguanea Club way *(Jamaica)*

4 servings:

breasts of 2 chickens	$\frac{1}{2}$ pint mayonnaise
1 lb. frozen chopped	(see page 35)
spinach or brocolli	2 dessertspoons curry
spears	powder
2 small tins cream of	breadcrumbs
chicken soup	Parmesan cheese, grated

Skin and bone and halve chicken breasts. Place a layer of spinach or brocolli in a casserole, put a layer of chicken on top; then a second layer of vegetable covered with remaining chicken.
Heat soup, undiluted. Add mayonnaise and curry powder and stir for a few seconds. Pour mixture into casserole, cover

with breadcrumbs and grated cheese. Place in a moderately hot oven (400°F. — Gas Mark 5) and cook for 45 minutes.

This is a very good main course for the cook-hostess, as it is a truly grand dish, fit for any dinner party. The recipe was given to me at the famous Liguanea Club on the outskirts of Kingston. No one who has visited this gracious white house with its pillared portico, cool veranda and swimming pool will forget it; if they had Liguanea chicken with the scent of flowers filling the open dining room, this too is something memorable.

Chicken Maryland *(St. Croix)*

4–6 servings:

1 3½-lb. chicken, jointed	1 egg, lightly beaten
milk	soft breadcrumbs
2 oz. flour	vegetable oil or fat for
salt	frying
pepper	

Dip chicken into milk. Sift flour and season well with salt and pepper. Dip chicken into flour, or shake in a paper bag to coat thoroughly. Dip into egg and breadcrumbs.
Heat 2-inches depth of oil or fat in a thick frying pan and brown chicken quickly all over. Cover pan and cook for 15–20 minutes. Uncover and cook for 15–20 minutes.*
Serve with savoury baked bananas (see page 82).

* cooking time depends on the thickness of the chicken joints

Chicken mould *(Jamaica)*

4 servings:

4 oz. rice, cooked and seasoned	chicken stock or milk
1 lb. chicken, skinned and boned	dash Worcestershire sauce
½ oz. butter	1 teaspoon parsley, chopped fine
4 oz. breadcrumbs	1 onion, minced
1 egg, beaten	salt
	pepper

Grease a pudding basin well, line with 1-inch thick wall of rice. Blend chicken with breadcrumbs, butter, egg, parsley, onion and sauce. Stir in enough chicken stock or milk to moisten. Place mixture in the bowl and cover with a thick layer of rice.

Cover the bowl with greaseproof paper tied down with string. Steam for 40 minutes, then turn on to a warm dish and serve with gravy made from chicken stock or tomato sherry sauce (see page 41).

Note:

This dish can be made with beef, veal, pork, rabbit or mutton used separately, together or mixed with chicken or any left-over meat.

Chicken paprika *(Bermuda)*

4 servings:

4 joints or quarters frying chicken	2 small green peppers, seeded and chopped finely
salt	¾ pint water or vegetable stock
2 oz. butter	¼ pint sour cream
4 medium onions, chopped	1 teaspoon flour
2 teaspoons paprika	boiled rice
6 medium tomatoes, chopped	

Skin chicken and sprinkle with salt. Melt butter and fry

onions until lightly browned. Add paprika, tomatoes, green peppers and stock and bring to the boil. Add chicken and cover closely.

Simmer gently for about 1½ hours, until chicken is very tender. Stir sour cream into flour smoothly, stir into the chicken pot a little at a time and simmer gently for 6–7 minutes. Serve hot, with rice.

Chicken with pineapple in the old style *(Cuba)*

6 servings:

6 joints or quarters of frying chicken	1 teaspoon brown sugar
lemon or lime juice	2 tomatoes, skinned and pulped
salt	
pepper	*For the sauce:*
flour	1 ripe pineapple, peeled and cored*
2 tablespoons butter	
1 onion, minced	1 tablespoon rum
3 tablespoons currants	
1 teaspoon lemon peel, finely grated	

Brush chicken with lemon juice, sprinkle with salt and pepper and dust in flour. Heat butter and brown chicken in it. Reduce heat and cover pan closely. Cook gently until chicken is tender. Then add onion, currants, lemon peel, brown sugar, tomatoes. Season to taste. Blend thoroughly and cook gently for a further 10 minutes.

Make the sauce: chop and crush pineapple and mix to a pulp with all its juice in an electric blender. Simmer until reduced to ¼ then stir in rum.

Pour sauce over chicken and serve.

* 1 12-oz. can pineapple may be substituted

Chicken Retreat Content *(Jamaica)*

4–6 servings:

1 large chicken, partly
  cooked
2 corn cobs
2 onions, chopped
2 tablespoons chopped
  chives
2 teaspoons parsley,
  chopped
sprig thyme

8 oz. string beans, cooked,
  or 1 can of beans
3 potatoes, partly cooked
  and sliced
dash Tobasco or
  Worcestershire sauce
salt
pepper
½ pint chicken stock or
  1 can chicken soup

Cut chicken into serving-sized pieces, cut sweet corn into 1-inch thick slices. Put into large saucepan, cover with stock. Add onions, chives, parsley, thyme and seasoning. Bring to boil, then simmer till onions are tender. Add beans, sliced potato and a little more stock or water to cover completely. Bring to boil and simmer, uncovered, for 3 minutes. Add sauce. The original recipe says 'serve in a wooden bowl or calabash', but soup plates or bowls do very nicely.

Retreat Content is a village in the parish of St. Mary in Jamaica; it would, at first glance, seem to be no more than a clearing in the mango, breadfruit and banana trees. But it has achieved fame by giving its name to this type of chicken stew which is known all over the island.

Chicken, New Providence style *(Bahamas)*

4 servings:

1 roasting chicken
1 small loaf bread, stale
salt
pinch thyme
black pepper
2 small onions, finely
  chopped

½ oz. butter
butter for basting
¾ pint water
1 tomato, peeled and
  chopped
4 potatoes, peeled and
  halved
dripping

Clean and dry chicken inside and out. Fork bread into crumbs and mix with a little salt, black pepper, onions and melted butter. Drop lightly into the bird without pressing in, reserving 4–5 tablespoons crumb mixture. Fold chicken legs, place in a large baking tin and sprinkle with salt. Dot generously with butter and surround chicken with remaining crumbs. Pour water over and add tomato.

Fry potatoes until crisp and golden in the dripping. Place around chicken and bake in a moderate oven (375° F. — Gas Mark 4) until chicken is tender and brown.

Note:
Add extra water during cooking if necessary

Chicken, spit roasted *(Basic method on several islands)*

4–6 servings:

1 roasting fowl	salt
2½ oz. butter	pepper
juice of 1 lime or ½ lemon	

Wipe chicken inside and out with a clean cloth. Mix butter with lime or lemon juice and a little salt and pepper. Put inside the bird, truss and impale it on the spit. Cook slowly over a hot fire of very dry wood with a pan under the turning bird. Baste, but not often as the skin should be crisp when cooked. When the bird is done, tip juice from inside it into pan, mix, strain and serve as gravy or a separate dip.

There are many variations such as stuffing the bird with a whole orange, skin slashed here and there, and serving a sauce of orange juice and honey.

Fresh tarragon leaves are sometimes put inside the bird, or it can be dusted with ground pimentos and quickly finished under the grill.

Sometimes barbecued chickens are served on a bed of fried plantains (see page 73) or fried slices of fresh pineapple. Barbecue sauce (see page 31) or Sherwood hot sauce (see page 40) are both suitable as 'dips'.

Cook-up *(British Guiana)*

4 servings:

4 oz. salt meat	pinch thyme
2 tablespoons oil	pinch parsley
2 teaspoons brown sugar	1 scallion, chopped
½ teaspoon salt	2 pints water
½ teaspoon pepper	1 lb. rice, well washed
1 onion, chopped	8 oz. cooked meat,
2 tomatoes, chopped	chopped

Wash and soak the salt meat. Heat oil and fry sugar until it bubbles. Add salt, pepper, onion, tomatoes, thyme, parsley and scallion. Fry until golden brown. Cube the salt meat and add to the pan with water and rice. Boil until rice is nearly cooked, stirring occasionally. Stir in cooked meat and continue cooking until rice is fluffy and the meat hot.

Curried goat *(Jamaica)*

4 servings:

1 oz. dripping	1 pint stock
1 lb. goat, mutton or lamb, cut in 1 inch cubes	1 tablespoon malt vinegar
	salt
2 large onions, peeled and finely sliced	pinch Cayenne pepper
	½ teaspoon allspice
2 teaspoons curry powder	¼ bay leaf
1 tablespoon coconut, freshly grated	2 dashes Tabasco
	boiled rice
½ teaspoon allspice	

Melt dripping and brown meat quickly. Remove, then cook onion in dripping until soft but not brown. Stir in curry powder, allspice and grated coconut. Cook, stirring, for a few moments, then stir in stock, vinegar, salt and Cayenne. Return meat to pan and simmer slowly for 2 hours. Add allspice and bay leaf about 30 minutes before the end of cooking. Just before serving, stir in Tabasco and serve surrounded by rice.

Goat water *(Montserrat)*

6–8 servings:

3 lb. goat meat, in 1-inch cubes	3 cloves
1 oz. butter	1 clove garlic, crushed
1 tablespoon tomato purée	½ oz. flour
1 large onion, chopped	salt
	1 teaspoon pepper

Put meat, butter, purée, onion, cloves, garlic, and most of the salt and pepper into a large saucepan; cover completely with cold water, bring to the boil and simmer for 2 hours. Mix flour with remaining salt and pepper, stir in enough water to make a thin paste. Stir this into the stew and cook till it thickens. Serve with rice and dasheen.*

* Dasheen looks like a turnip with broad green leaves; it is not essential if it does not grow around your way! Mutton may be substituted for goat and less pepper used for a milder stew.

Note:

In Montserrat, a tiny island, 15 minutes away from Antigua, everyone serves goat water at weddings, christenings and house warmings, known on the island as a 'house maroon'. Probably a strong local rum will be drunk with it, called 'plastic' in these parts. I got this information with the recipe from Mrs. Peters, smiling owner of the Emerald Isle Hotel; she told me that Montserrat is called the Emerald Isle of the Caribbean, not only because it is so green and fertile, but because many of the inhabitants are of Irish descent. Although it is so near to Antigua, it is completely different as indeed, are all the islands of the Caribbean. Antigua is flat and rather bleak but ringed with wonderful white sand beaches; Montserrat is green and hilly and has black sand beaches. Everywhere the immortelle trees drop their red and yellow bird-shaped flowers through which the children whistle, making a sound like a bird.

Grapefruit basted bacon *(Barbados)*

4–6 servings:

1 forehock of bacon, par-boiled	1 grapefruit
¼ pint grapefruit juice	brown sugar
	cinnamon

Place bacon in a baking dish and pour grapefruit juice over. Bake in a very moderate oven (350° F. — Gas Mark 3) for about 30 minutes, basting frequently.
Cut grapefruit into 6, dip in sugar, then cinnamon and brown under a hot grill. Serve bacon garnished with grapefruit.

Grilled steak with rum butter, Port Antonio style *(Jamaica)*

4 servings:

3 tablespoons rum	2 teaspoons fresh lime or lemon juice
1 tablespoon shallots, finely chopped	1 tablespoon parsley, chopped
3 oz. butter	salt and pepper
	rump steak for 4 servings

Pour rum into a pan, stir in shallots, season well. Bring to the boil and simmer until ⅔ reduced. Allow to cool slightly. While still warm, stir in butter, juice and parsley, beating well to blend. Allow to cool, then put in the refrigerator.
  Grill steaks to taste, serve with rum butter on top of each.

Island fritters *(Tortola)*

4–6 servings:

4 oz. flour	1¼ lb. bacon or ham, minced
salt	6 slices grapefruit, peeled
pepper	fat for frying
3 eggs	
4 tablespoons milk	

Sift flour with salt and pepper. Make a well in the centre and work in eggs, one at a time, followed by milk, added gradually. Beat until very smooth and leave to stand for about 30 minutes.

Mix half the batter with bacon or ham. Dip grapefruit slices in remaining half. Drop meat mixture, by spoon, into boiling fat and fry until golden. Drop coated grapefruit slices into fat and fry until crisp. Serve grapefruit fritters topped by meat.

Lamb curry *(Bahamas)*

4 servings:

2 tablespoons butter	water
2 onions, thinly sliced	1 oz. flour
1 tablespoon curry powder	salt
1 green pepper, chopped	pepper
1 cooking apple, peeled,	grated fresh coconut
cored and thinly sliced	tomato slices
1½ lb. lamb or mutton,	mango chutney
or any diced meat	(see page 221)
	boiled rice

Melt butter and sauté onions until lightly browned. Add curry powder, green pepper and apple and fry until tender, stirring occasionally with a wooden spoon. Add meat and brown all over lightly. Cover with boiling water and simmer gently until meat is tender. Season flour well with salt and pepper and mix to a thin paste with cold water. Stir into curry and stir over a low heat until thick. Cook for 6–7 minutes. Serve hot, with plenty of grated coconut, sliced tomato and mango chutney on a bed of rice.

Note:

Stoned raisins may be added and mango chutney (see page 221) served with it.

Lemon lamb *(Aruba)*

4 servings:

juice of 4 limes or
   2 lemons
2 tablespoons olive oil
2 tablespoons onion,
   grated
1 tablespoon chilli powder
2 teaspoons curry powder
2 teaspoons ground
   ginger
2 teaspoons tumeric

1 clove garlic, crushed
1 teaspoon salt
2 lb. lamb cut into
   1½ inch cubes
4 onions, quartered
6 slices pineapple, halved
4 tomatoes, quartered
8 slices bacon, halved
1 green pepper

Combine juice, olive oil, grated onion, chilli powder, curry powder, ginger, tumeric, garlic and salt. Blend well, then add lamb cubes and leave to marinate overnight in a cool place.

Put marinated meat on to long skewers alternating with pieces of onion, pineapple, tomato and bacon slices wrapped round pieces of green pepper. Place skewers on rack under the grill about 3 ins. from the flame; grill for 15 to 20 minutes, turning often to brown all sides.

Serve with a dip of peanut butter sauce, (see page 36).

This kebab dish, known as 'lamchi and boonchi' in the Netherlands Antilles, makes an excellent barbecue dish.

Mould of lamb *(Grenada)*

4 servings:

½ oz. gelatine
1 pint water
1 teaspoon fresh lime or
   lemon juice
2 tablespoons vinegar
2 teaspoons sugar
1 teaspoon salt

8 oz. lamb, cooked and
   sliced
4 oz. young cabbage,
   finely chopped
1 tablespoon peas, cooked
grated nutmeg
1 lettuce

Dissolve gelatine in water, adding the juice, vinegar, sugar and salt. Strain, allow to cool; when beginning to set add the lamb, cabbage, peas and nutmeg. Pour into a wet mould and allow to set. Chill and turn on to a bed of lettuce.

Pepper-pot (Antigua)

4 servings:

8 oz. salt pork, pig snout or pig trotters	4 tablespoons pumpkin, diced
8 oz. salt beef	2 tomatoes, chopped
8 oz. fresh meat	4 tablespoons squash, diced
water	salt
4 eddo leaves, optional,	pepper
4 aubergines, diced	bunch chives
4 okra, diced	sprig thyme
2 onions, chopped	1 lb. green peas, cooked
1 lb. spinach, chopped	

Wash and chop meats, bring to the boil in plenty of water. Skim and simmer gently until nearly cooked. Cut eddo leaves into small pieces and add to meat with aubergines, okra, onions, spinach, pumpkin, tomatoes and squash. Season well and cook until thick. Add chives and flavour with thyme. Stir in peas and return to a low heat for 5–6 minutes. Serve very hot.

Pepper-pot *(British Guiana)*

6-8 servings

1 oxtail or calf's head or boiling fowl	2-3 tablespoons brown sugar
2 lb. lean pork	¼ pint cassereep*
4 red peppers	2 onions
bunch thyme	

Cube meat, put into a large casserole, cover with cold water and simmer till nearly cooked, about 1½ hours.
Chop peppers, thyme and onions and add to meat with sugar and cassareep. Simmer until meat is quite tender and a thick sauce has formed.

* No true pepper pot can be made without cassereep, a West Indian product made from cassava juice. No flour or starch should be added to the true pepper pot as this would turn it sour. It is rather like a French 'pot au feu', should be re-heated daily to keep it good and the pot should almost never be rinsed out.
If cassareep is not available, substitute stock and make this recipe as a pleasant hot tasting stew.

Note:
Pepper pot, as made in British Guiana, Barbados and other islands in the Lesser Antilles, is a stew and should not be confused with pepper pot soup, which is Jamaican.

Pineapple spareribs *(St. Vincent)*

4-6 servings:

2 lb. spareribs	¼ pint oil
3 pints water	1 large can pineapple cubes
¾ pint cider vinegar	
3 oz. cornflour	4 oz. sugar
2 tablespoons black molasses	2 green peppers, seeded and diced

140

Cut ribs into individual chops. Bring 2½ pints water to the boil and stir in ¼ pint vinegar. Add ribs, bring to the boil and simmer gently for 15 minutes. Drain. Sift cornflour and stir in molasses. Coat ribs and brown in oil.

In a deep pan, stir together ¼ pint pineapple juice and remaining water and vinegar. Add sugar, then heat, stirring until dissolved. Bring to the boil and add spareribs. Cover closely and simmer gently for 30 minutes, turning the ribs often. Add pineapple cubes and green pepper and simmer for 5–6 minutes. Serve very hot.

Port Royal lamb stew *(Jamaica)*

4 servings:

1½ lb. boneless stewing lamb	2 oz. butter or dripping
salt	½ oz. flour
pepper	1 egg yolk, beaten
1 bay leaf	1 teaspoon orange rind, finely grated
1 tablespoon vinegar	4 oz. mushrooms, cooked
1½ pints beef stock or water	dash Angostura bitters
	boiled rice

Cut meat into 1-inch cubes, removing fat. Sprinkle with salt and pepper, add bay leaf and stir in vinegar and stock. Bring to the boil and simmer gently, covered, for 1 hour, or until tender. Strain and allow stock to cool slightly.

Meanwhile make a roux by melting butter and stirring in flour. Cook for a few moments, stirring, then remove from heat and gradually stir in warm stock. Stir in egg yolk, cook and stir until mixture thickens. Continue cooking gently for about 5 minutes. Add lamb, orange peel, mushrooms and bitters.

Heat through over a low heat and serve hot with rice.

Roast leg of lamb, à la Criolla *(Puerto Rico)*

6–8 servings:

4–5 lb. leg of lamb	1 teaspoon oregano
1 clove garlic, chopped	1½ tablespoons olive oil
¼ teaspoon black pepper	4 teaspoons salt
	extra pepper

Remove skin and excess fat, wipe meat with a damp cloth. Place on a rack in a shallow pan, fat side up. Carefully make superficial criss-cross cuts on top of the joint. Crush garlic, pepper and oregano together in a small bowl, using a wooden spoon. Add olive oil, salt and extra pepper and blend well. Rub into meat, cover and put in the refrigerator overnight.

Take out 30 minutes before required for cooking and drain off any liquid. Pour this back over the joint, then roast, uncovered, in a very moderate oven (350° F. — Gas Mark 3) allowing 35–40 minutes per pound. Use the pan drippings to make gravy.

Roast sucking pig *(Jamaica)*

12 servings or more according to size of pig:

4–6 lb. prepared sucking pig (about 3 weeks old)	1 clove garlic, crushed
	½ teaspoon allspice
6 oz. breadcrumbs	1 teaspoon thyme, chopped
milk	salt
1 tablespon capers, chopped	black pepper
6-8 olives, chopped	1 large potato, baked
4 oz. small peas, cooked and crushed	butter for basting

Wash pig in cold water, dry with a clean cloth. Loosen the skin round the trotters, fold back over the ends and cut off the trotters. Stuff the belly with a paste made from breacrumbs, moistened with milk, capers, olives, peas, garlic, allspice, thyme, salt and pepper. Sew up belly, rub a little salt over the pig. Brush with melted butter, draw the legs back and tie with string.

Wrap in double foil or greaseproof paper, bake in a moderately hot oven (400°F. — Gas Mark 5) for 2½ to 3 hours.

Remove paper and roast for the last ½ hour without, dredging with flour and basting all the time.

Place potato in the pig's mouth and serve with gravy, Creole sauce or Salamagundi sauce (see pages 32, 38).

Salt beef ad red peas *(Jamaica)*

4–6 servings:

1½ lb. salt beef	2 scallions, chopped
½ pint red peas, or kidney beans	½ oz. butter
	1 tablespoon cornmeal
salt	cornmeal dumpling
pepper	batter (see page 47)
dash Tabasco	boiled rice
¼ teaspoon thyme	

Soak beef in water for 12 hours. Drain and bring to the boil in fresh water. Simmer until tender. Meanwhile, bring red peas to boil in plenty of water and cook slowly until tender, about 3 hours. Add to beef, season to taste, add a good dash of Tabasco, thyme and scallions. Melt butter and stir in cornmeal. Dilute with a little cooled stock from beef pot and, when mixed to a thin, smooth paste, stir into beef mixture. Stir until thickened.

Drop in dumpling batter formed into small balls and cover closely. Simmer gently for 20–30 minutes, until dumplings are cooked.

Serve with rice.

Scalloped sweetbreads and mushrooms *(Bermuda)*

4 servings:

1 lb. sweetbreads	1 can mushrooms or ¼ lb.
1 tablespoon lemon or	fresh mushrooms,
lime juice	cooked
1 oz. butter	¼ pint stock
2 shallots, minced or	1 pimento, shredded finely
finely chopped	1 teaspoon sweet green
½ clove garlic, crushed	pepper, finely chopped
¼ teaspoon Cayenne	salt
1 oz. flour	3 oz. breadcrumbs
¾ pint milk	butter

Soak sweetbreads for 45 minutes in cold water. Drain and cover with boiling salted water. Add the juice and simmer gently for 15 minutes. Drain and immediately plunge into cold water. Remove membranes and break into pieces.

Heat butter and sauté shallots, garlic and Cayenne gently for 5 minutes. Stir in flour, blend thoroughly, then gradually stir in milk. Drain mushrooms and stir the liquid and stock into sauce. Stir until thickened. Add pimento and green pepper and salt to taste. Simmer gently for 5 minutes.

Arrange sweetbreads in a buttered casserole, sprinkle with mushrooms and 1½ oz. breadcrumbs. Pour over sauce, sprinkle with remaining breadcrumbs and dot with butter. Bake in a very moderate oven (350° F. — Gas Mark 3) for 25 minutes.

Smoked meat *(Used on many West Indian islands)*

small joints of meat	salt

Clean meat and rub well with plenty of salt. Hang it over a slow fire made from green or slightly damp wood. Turn constantly until all sides are well smoked. Leave it hanging over a wood fire and smoke it daily for several days.
When using, cut meat from the lower end and smoke the cut end again.

This is the original method used by the 'bouccaniers' mentioned in the Introduction. It is not especially nice, unless very tender cuts are used, as it is inclined to make the meat dry and rather tough.

Spiced barbecued meat *(Surinam)*

4 servings:

4 small onions, very finely minced	1½ teaspoons curry powder
2 cloves garlic, ground fine	½ teaspoon ground cloves
1 teaspoon Cayenne pepper	½ teaspoon ground ginger
½ oz. brown sugar	3 tablespoons water
1 teaspoon fresh lime or lemon juice	1½ oz. melted butter
	1½ lbs. steak*

*Thick skirt is suitable, quite tender once it is marinated

Blend onions, garlic, Cayenne, sugar, juice and spices, then add water. Put in meat and knead with the hands so that it absorbs the liquid. Put in the refrigerator for 6 hours. Take 4 or 8 skewers, according to their length, thread cubes of meat on, brush with melted butter. Put on a rack under the grill, about 3 inches from heat. Turn, brushing frequently with butter and cook for 15–20 minutes, making sure all sides are exposed to heat. Serve with peanut butter sauce see page 36).

This is part of the 'Very small rice table' of Surinam. Originally the Rijsttafel of the Netherlands East Indies was a vast table loaded with dishes, a huge rice bowl in the centre. To eat it took most of the afternoon. Surinamese have simplified the Rijsttafel to only eight dishes, all on the hot and spicy side. They serve strips of cucumber and banana to take away the hot taste. Very little salt is used in accordance with East Indian cooking procedure.

Spit roasted sucking pig (*Jamaica*):

12–18 servings according to size of pig:

4–6 lb. sucking pig, prepared	black pepper
2 onions, chopped fine	1 gill rum
chives, chopped fine	parsley, chopped
butter	clove garlic, crushed
8 oz. breadcrumbs	2 limes or 1 lemon, cut
milk	oil for basting
salt	4 oranges

Remove offal; mince heart, tongue, liver and spleen (melt) finely. Fry onion in butter until tender, add chives when about half cooked. Mix breadcrumbs to a paste with milk, add salt and pepper, cooked onions and chives, rum, parsley and garlic.

Blend all well, then stuff into the belly; sew up the slit rub all over with lemon or lime. Brush with oil, put pig on the spit and cook over a very hot fire of dry wood, basting all the time with oil*. The pig will take 1¾–3 hours, according to size. Peel oranges, scrape and slice, serve with the pig.

* This is better than lard as the crackling will be crisper

In Jamaica, this is the traditional New Year's Eve party dish; it is said that if the first morsel eaten after the New Year comes in, is sucking pig, the year will be a very lucky one.

Souse (*Several West Indian islands use this dish*):

4–6 servings:

½ pig's head	1 tablespoon salt
1 pig's tongue	1 green pepper, seeded and chopped
2 pig's trotters	1 slice cucumber
lime juice or lemon juice, freshly squeezed	¼ pint stock

Scald and scrape meats. Wash thoroughly with lime or lemon juice. Tie in a floured cloth, place in a large pan, cover with cold water and bring to the boil. Simmer very gently until tender, about 1½ hours. Allow to cool in the liquid.

Remove and untie the meat. Skin and slice the tongue, slice meat from the head and cut open the trotters. Place all meat in a deep dish, sprinkle with 2 teaspoons salt, juice of 4 limes or 3 lemons, and enough cold water to cover. Stand for 12 hours. Drain and wash the meat.

Make a sauce with the juice of 2 limes or lemons, remaining salt, green pepper, cucumber and stock; serve with meat.

Steak and kidney pudding *(Bermuda)*

6–8 servings :

For the dough:

1½ lb. flour	12 oz. chopped suet
½ oz. baking powder	cold water
½ teaspoon salt	

For the filling:

2 lb. lean beef, diced	2 oz. flour
1 beef kidney, diced	2 teaspoons salt
1 large onion, chopped finely	3 tablespoons Worcestershire sauce
1 clove garlic, crushed	¾ pint water

Make the dough: sift flour, baking powder and salt and mix suet in. Add cold water to make a stiff dough. Knead lightly and roll out about ⅔ dough to ¼ inch thick. Line a large pudding basin with it.

Make the filling: mix beef and kidney. Mix onion and garlic. Arrange meat and onion in alternate layers in the lined basin, dredging each layer with flour and seasoning. Mix sauce and water and pour in. Roll out remaining dough to ¼ inch thick and cover pudding, sealing edges with water. Cover with foil or well-greased paper and tie basin in a clean white cloth. Steam for 4 hours.

Steamed wild hog *(Bahamas)*

4–6 servings:

2 lb. wild hog meat
salted water
lard
2 onions, sliced
2 oz. butter
2 tablespoons tomato
  purée

black pepper
salt
2 tablespoons orange
  juice
2 teaspoons orange rind,
  finely grated
12 coriander seeds,
  crushed

Bone meat then chop into 2-inch cubes; place in a pan with bones and cover with salted water. Simmer gently until meat is tender, about 1½ hours. Drain, reserving ⅓ pint liquid.
Sauté meat in lard until brown, fry onion in butter until tender. Stir tomato purée, into butter, season, then add orange juice, rind and coriander seeds. Add reserved liquid and cook until sauce is reduced and thickened.
Add meat and cook for 10 minutes over a gentle heat.

Note:
This method is very good with oxtail but leave the meat on the bones.

Stuffed guinea hen *(Haiti)*

4 servings:

1 guinea hen
4 oz. breadcrumbs,
  coarse
fat for deep frying
salt
Cayenne pepper
juice of 2 limes
  or 1 lemon

rind of 1 lime
  or ½ lemon, grated
1 teaspoon brown sugar
¼ teaspoon nutmeg,
  grated
3 tablespoons rum
2–3 bananas, mashed
butter

Clean hen well. Fry breadcrumbs until golden in hot deep fat.

148

Drain, then season well. Stir in juice, rind, sugar, nutmeg and 1 tablespoon rum. The mixture should be a stiff paste, so add more juice if required. Stuff this into the bird's breast and fill tail end cavity with banana. Sew up and roast in a hot oven (400°F. — Gas Mark 5) for about 35–40 minutes, basting all the time with butter.

Heat remaining rum and, just before the bird is taken to the table, pour over and set it alight.

Note:

An excellent garnish for this dish is guava cheese (see page 220). This is one of the best dishes I encountered on my travels and it is really very easy to prepare. Guava cheese can be bought in Oriental stores.

Sweet and sour beef *(Curaçao)*

6–8 servings:

1½ lb. sirloin steak	¾ pint water
2 eggs	⅓ pint vinegar
1 clove garlic, crushed	4 oz. brown sugar
2 oz. cornflour	1 teaspoon salt
fat for deep frying	2 green peppers, seeded
1–8 oz. can pineapple	and cut in strips
chunks or fresh	2 tomatoes, coarsely
pineapple pieces*	chopped

* If fresh pineapple is used, boil with a little water and sugar and allow to cool before using.

Cut meat into ½-inch cubes. Whisk eggs and beat in garlic. Dip meat in this and then into 1 oz. cornflour. Heat the fat to 375°F. and fry meat for 3–4 minutes, until well browned. Drain on absorbent paper.

Drain pineapple and reserve chunks. Stir juice into remaining cornflour, then water, vinegar, sugar and salt Turn into a pan and cook slowly, stirring all the time. Add beef, pineapple chunks, green peppers and tomatoes and heat through gently for 4 minutes. Serve very hot.

Sweet and sour pork, Alcoa method *(Trinidad)*

4 servings:

4 tablespoons water
3 tablespoons vinegar
2 oz. brown sugar
1 oz. cornflour
½ teaspoon salt
8 oz. can pineapple
   chunks, or pieces
   fresh pineapple*

1½ lb. cooked pork, sliced
melted dripping
1 green pepper,
   thinly sliced
2 onions, thinly sliced

Mix water, vinegar, sugar, cornflour and salt with 8 table-spoons pineapple juice drained from the can. Cook, stirring, until clear and slightly thickened. Brown meat in dripping, pour over sauce and cook for 30 minutes. Add pineapple chunks, green pepper and onion and cook for 2 minutes.

* If fresh pineapple is used, boil in a little water to which sugar has been added. Allow to cool, then use as for canned fruit.

Desserts and puddings

In the West Indies, obviously bananas, citrus fruits, pineapple, coffee and rum figure very often in the sweets. About the most popular dessert right through the islands is some form of baked bananas, with or without rum. Strangely enough, in this hot climate, steamed puddings and pies are very frequently served. The recipes using sweet potatoes can be tried in Britain and, although some of the rum recipes are sophisticated, such sweets as baked oranges are quite suitable for family meals and make a welcome difference. Yoghurt ice in the simpler version is also an original everyday sweet. On most of the islands I have visited the population has a very sweet tooth.

Avocado ice-cream *(Jamaica)*

approx. 6–8 servings:

2 eggs	½ teaspoon vanilla or
8 oz. sugar	almond essence, optional
1 pint milk	2 medium-sized
	avocado pears

Beat eggs lightly and add 4 oz. sugar and milk. Cook in a double boiler, stirring, until the custard thickens. Add essence and allow to cool. Mix remaining sugar with peeled, stoned and mashed pears and beat well. Thoroughly blend pear mixture into custard, turn into a freezing tray and freeze to a mush. Remove from refrigerator, beat again and return to freezing compartment set at lowest.

Banana and grape salad

4 servings:

2 oranges	2 pineapple rings,
4 oz. grapes	canned or fresh
4 ripe bananas	whipped cream

Peel oranges and remove pith. Chop into small pieces and lay these in a shallow fruit bowl. Halve grapes and remove pips. Peel bananas and halve lengthways. Cut halves across 3 times and arrange these and grapes over oranges. Cut each pineapple ring into 6 and arrange in a ring on the other fruit and chill. Serve with whipped cream.

Banana and orange meringue

4–6 servings:

2 oz. brown sugar
5 ripe bananas
2 oranges
1 tablespoon lemon
or lime juice

2 egg whites
1 oz. castor sugar
whipped cream

Sprinkle 1 oz. brown sugar evenly over the bottom of a shallow pie dish. Peel bananas and cut in half lengthwise and then across. Arrange on top of sugar with the peel of 1 orange finely grated. Remove peel and pith from both oranges and slice thinly; lay these on top of bananas, put remaining brown sugar on top and sprinkle with lemon or lime juice. Beat egg whites, add castor sugar a little at a time and continue beating until stiff. Pile on top of fruit.
Bake in a moderate oven (350° F. — Gas Mark 3) for 15 minutes. Allow to cool, serve chilled with whipped cream or coconut cream (see page 42).

Bananas au rum flambée *(Antigua)*

4–6 servings:

6 oz. brown sugar
1 oz. butter, melted
milk

6 bananas sliced
lengthwise
½ pint rum

Add sugar to butter with enough milk to blend, and bring to the boil. Allow to cool. Place bananas in a greased fire-proof dish, cook in a moderate oven (350° F. — Gas Mark 3) for 15 minutes. Just before fruit is cooked, bring sugar mixture again to the boil, add ¼ pint rum, pour over bananas. Heat remaining rum, pour over just before serving and set alight.

Although this recipe was given to me at the Admiral's Inn, Antigua, I have had it in many places in the West Indies. It is one of the most popular desserts.

Bananas baked *(Jamaica)*

4 servings:

4 bananas	½ teaspoon allspice
1½ oz. brown sugar	½ gill rum
2 tablespoons lemon or lime juice	3 tablespoons cold water

Peel and cut bananas, halve lengthwise. Place in a well greased pudding basin. Sprinkle with sugar, pour juice and rum over fruit, then sprinkle with allspice, dot with butter and add water. Bake in a moderate oven (350°F. — Gas Mark 3) for 45 minutes, turning the fruit from time to time.

This is served all over Jamaica and very often on the other islands.

Banana casserole *(Grenada)*

4–6 servings:

6 bananas, quartered	¼ teaspoon powdered clove
1 tablespoon lemon juice	1½ teaspoons orange peel, grated
1 oz. butter	
pinch salt	2 tablespoons macaroons, crushed
¼ pint red cooking wine	
8 oz. brown sugar	1 tablespoon almonds, chopped
1 teaspoon cinnamon	
1 teaspoon nutmeg	

Brush banana pieces with lemon juice and fry lightly in butter to which salt has been added. Heat wine, sugar, cinnamon, nutmeg, clove and orange peel and simmer gently until syrupy. Arrange bananas in a buttered dish, pour syrup over and sprinkle mixed macaroons and almonds on. Cook for 15–20 minutes in a moderate oven (350°F. — Gas Mark 3) until the top is nicely browned.
Just before serving, heat rum, pour over bananas, set alight and serve.

Bananas Celeste *(Martinique)*

4–6 servings:

6 bananas, peeled and
  halved lengthways
2 oz. butter
8 oz. cream cheese

2 oz. brown sugar
½ teaspoon cinnamon
3 tablespoons thick
  cream or yoghurt

Brown halved bananas in butter and arrange 6 pieces in a buttered pie plate. Cream the cream cheese, sugar and cinnamon and spread half the mixture on bananas. Add another layer of bananas, another layer of cheese mixture and pour cream or yoghurt over the top. Bake in a moderate oven (375° F. — Gas Mark 4) for 20 minutes.

Banana dessert omelette

2–4 servings:

1½ oz. fresh breadcrumbs
2 tablespoons thin cream
2 eggs, separated
¾ teaspoon salt
1 oz. sugar

½ teaspoon vanilla
  essence, if liked
2 or 3 bananas,
  chopped
1 oz. butter

Stir breadcrumbs into cream and soak for 5 minutes. Beat yolks and stir into breadcrumbs with salt, sugar and vanilla. Add bananas, and fold in the stiffly beaten egg whites. Melt butter in a 9-inch baking pan and turn the mixture into it. Cook for 10 minutes in a moderate oven (375° F. — Gas Mark 4) when the omelette will be lightly browned and puffy.

Bananas, fried *(Barbados)*

4–6 servings:

6–8 bananas
3 oz. butter

juice of 1 lemon
1 oz. Demerara sugar

Peel bananas and place whole in 1½ oz. melted butter in a large frying pan. Sprinkle with lemon juice, dot with remaining butter and top with sugar. Cook over a low heat until soft and serve with raisin sauce (see page 43).

Banana fritters *(Jamaica)*

4 servings:

3 ripe bananas
1 egg
½ oz. sugar

1½ oz. flour
½ teaspoon baking powder
icing sugar

Peel and mash bananas to a smooth pulp. Beat egg and sugar together and blend into banana pulp. Sift flour and baking powder and add, a little at a time, to banana mixture, stirring in well. Drop by dessertspoonfuls on to a hot greased griddle or a hot, oiled frying pan. Sprinkle with icing sugar and serve with coconut cream (see page 42).

Banana Frost-and-Fire *(Bahamas)*

4 servings:

2 egg whites (3, if small eggs)
1½ tablespoons castor sugar
3 bananas

1 block of ice cream, preferably coffee, frozen very hard
1½ tablespoons rum

Stiffly beat the whites, and sugar a little at a time and beat until very stiff indeed. Peel and halve bananas lengthwise, then cut each half into 3. Arrange half the banana pieces in an oven-proof dish to form an oblong a little larger than the ice cream. Place ice cream on the bananas and cover with remaining banana. Spoon the egg white over so it completely covers and seals the ice cream and prevents it from touching the dish. Pre-heat the oven to very hot (450° F. — Gas Mark 8) and quickly bake for about 4 minutes.

While it is baking, warm the rum. Take the dish from the oven, pour rum over and set it alight. Serve flaming.

Banana ice-cream

6–8 servings:

1 14-oz. can evaporated milk	juice of 1 fresh lime or lemon
$\frac{1}{2}$ pint milk	1 teaspoon vanilla essence
4 oz. sugar	essence
2 eggs, separated	pinch salt
2 mashed bananas	chopped nuts

Heat milks and sugar until almost boiling. Pour, stirring, on to beaten egg yolks and return to heat. Stir all the time until custard thickens. Do not allow to boil. Cool and stir in bananas, lime juice and essence. Whisk egg whites with salt until stiff, stir into mixture. Turn into the freezing tray and freeze until mushy. Remove and beat thoroughly before returning to freezing compartment set at coldest.

Bananas in skins *(Jamaica)*

6 servings:

4 tablespoons rum	6 bananas, firm and with good skins
$\frac{1}{4}$ pint thick cream	sugar to taste

Whip rum with cream. Split each banana lengthwise and remove fruit without tearing the skins. Mash fruit, mix in rum and cream and sweeten to taste. Pack mixture into skins. Set for a few minutes in a hot oven (400° F. — Gas Mark 4). Serve very hot.

Banana nut pudding *(Tobago)*

4 servings:

4 slices ½ inch thick bread, thinly buttered	2 teaspoons lemon or lime rind, finely grated
4 oz. chopped nuts	2 eggs
4 bananas, peeled	¾ pint milk
2 oz. sugar	pinch grated nutmeg

Remove crusts and dice bread. Butter a shallow pie dish, place a layer of bread in the bottom, sprinkle with 2 oz. nuts. Cover with sliced banana, cut across. Add 1 oz. sugar and all lemon or lime rind. Cover with remaining nuts, then the bread.

Beat eggs with remaining sugar, stir in milk and pour over the bread. Grate a little nutmeg over the top. Bake in a moderate oven (350°F. — Gas Mark 3) for 35 minutes until it sets.

Serve with coconut cream (see page 42) or whipped cream.

Banana pancakes

4 servings:

basic pancake batter (see page 179)

For the filling:

4 small, ripe bananas	grated rind and juice of 1 lemon or 2 limes
1 oz. soft brown sugar	extra sugar

Make the pancakes and keep warm. Slice bananas very thinly and mix with sugar, rind and juice. Fill pancakes with this and sprinkle with a little more brown sugar before serving.

Banana pudding, Elbow Beach style *(Bermuda)*

4–8 servings:

1 oz. butter	1 oz. flour
2 oz. brown sugar	4 tablespoons milk
8 bananas, peeled and mashed	whipped cream

Cream butter and sugar and beat in bananas. Add flour and milk, alternately, a little at a time. Turn into a buttered 9-ins. pie dish, and bake for 45 minutes in a moderate oven (375° F. — Gas Mark 4). Serve hot with cream.

Banana pumpkin pie *(Bermuda)*

6–8 servings:

2 bananas, peeled and mashed	$\frac{1}{4}$ teaspoon nutmeg
4 rounded tablespoons pumpkin, cooked and mashed	$\frac{1}{8}$ teaspoon ground cloves
1 tablespoon fresh lemon or lime juice	3 eggs, separated
4 oz. sugar	$\frac{1}{2}$ oz. gelatine
$\frac{1}{4}$ teaspoon salt	1 9-inch pie shell, baked blind (see page 160)
	whipped cream

Mix bananas, pumpkin, lemon or lime juice, 2 oz. sugar, salt, nutmeg, cloves and lightly beaten egg yolks. Stirring all the time, cook over a gentle heat for 5 minutes, until mixture is slightly thickened. Remove from heat and stir in gelatine, dissolved in a little water. Cool.

Beat egg whites until foamy and add remaining sugar a little at a time, beating thoroughly. Continue beating until mixture is very stiff, then fold in banana mixture carefully. Turn into the cooled pie shell and chill until firm. Serve cold with cream.

Banana pasties in sharp sauce *(St. Kitts)*

4 servings:

4 bananas	pinch cinnamon
1 oz. castor sugar	8 oz. short pastry
	(see below)

For the sauce:

8 oz. castor sugar	juice of 1 lemon
2 teaspoons cornflour	or 2 limes
$\frac{1}{4}$ pint water, boiling	finely grated lemon
pinch salt	or lime peel

Halve bananas, roll each half firmly in sugar mixed with cinnamon. Roll out pastry, cut into oblongs and wrap round each banana piece. Bake on a floured baking sheet in a moderate oven (350° F. — Gas Mark 3) for 15 minutes.

To make the sauce:
Mix sugar and cornflour, stir in boiling water slowly. Bring to the boil and cook over a gentle heat, stirring all the time. Remove from heat, stir in salt, juice and rind.
Serve sauce and pasties hot or cold.

Pastry, short crust

8 oz. plain or self-raising flour
  pinch salt
4 oz. butter or margarine
2 tablespoons cold water

Sieve the flour and salt into a mixing bowl. Cut the butter or margarine into four and rub into the flour until mixture looks like fine breadcrumbs. Add the water and mix until it clings together. Gather together with the finger-tips to form a firm dough. Lightly flour the rolling-pin and board. Roll the pastry out to the required thickness with light, quick, forward strokes. Cut and use the pastry as directed in the recipe used.

Bananas, roasted in mountain style *(Jamaica)*

bananas
sugar

lime or lemon
juice

Leave ripe bananas unpeeled and put into the ashes under a good fire. Roast for about 30 minutes when they should look black.
Run a fork down each banana and lay it open. Dust with sugar, squeeze a little fresh lime or lemon juice over and eat with a spoon and fork or in the fingers.

This is a very good outdoor sweet, to be cooked at a picnic.

Banana rum fritters

4 servings:

4 bananas
1 oz. sugar

$\frac{1}{2}$ gill rum

For the batter:

1 gill warm water
3 oz. plain flour   2 egg whites
pinch salt
1 tablespoon olive oil

deep fat for frying   castor sugar

Peel and cut bananas into $\frac{1}{2}$-inch thick rounds. Lay rounds in a shallow dish, sprinkle with sugar and pour rum on. Allow to stand for $1\frac{1}{2}$ hours, turning from time to time.
Prepare the batter: sift flour and salt together. Make a well in the centre and pour in oil and water gradually. Mix to a smooth batter and leave to stand for 1 hour. Just before it is needed, lightly fold in the stiffly beaten egg whites.
Drop banana rounds in singly, so they are completely coated. Fry in deep fat which has been heated so that a faint blue smoke rises. Drain on paper and serve immediately sprinkled with castor sugar.

Bluebeard's rum custard pudding
(U. S. Virgin Islands)

5 servings:

5 eggs	$\frac{3}{4}$ pint milk
1 oz. brown sugar	2 tablespoons rum
$\frac{1}{2}$ oz. cornflour	

Beat eggs well, stir in sugar and cornflour. Bring milk to the boil and, stirring all the time, slowly pour in egg mixture. Continue cooking over a very gentle heat, stirring constantly until custard thickens. Remove from heat, stir in rum and pour into individual glasses. Chill and serve very cold.

Carrot pudding *(Bahamas)*

6–8 servings:

6 oz. butter	1 teaspoon baking powder
6 oz. seedless raisins, chopped	pinch salt
8 oz. carrots, peeled and grated	6 oz. soft brown sugar
	$\frac{1}{4}$ teaspoon grated nutmeg
5 oz. flour	$\frac{1}{2}$ teaspoon powdered cinnamon

Cream the butter, stir in raisins and carrots. Sift flour and mix with remaining ingredients. Work into carrot mixture and press into a shallow baking dish. Bake in a very moderate oven (350°F. — Gas Mark 3), for about 40 minutes.

Note:
This is delicious with cream.

Chilled ginger cream *(Trinidad)*

2–4 servings:

2 eggs	1 tablespoon water
2 tablespoons castor	1 gill whipped cream
sugar	4 tablespoons rum
1 gill milk	2 oz. preserved
¼ oz. gelatine	ginger, chopped

Separate eggs and stir sugar into yolks. Blend thoroughly. Bring milk just to the boil and pour steadily into yolk mixture, stirring all the time. Heat in a double boiler until thickened, but do not allow to boil. Remove from heat and stir in gelatine dissolved in water. Strain and stand in a cool place until just on the point of setting. Fold in cream, stiffly beaten egg whites, rum and ginger. Turn into a prepared mould and chill in the refrigerator until the cream has set.

Coconut pudding *(Bahamas)*

6–8 servings:

4 egg yolks	1 coconut, grated,
1 pint milk	or 1 packet dessicated
8 oz. sugar	coconut
1 teaspoon lemon or lime	4 oz. breadcrumbs
juice	

For meringue topping:

4 egg whites	2 oz. sugar

Beat yolks until light, stir in milk, sugar and juice, then coconut and breadcrumbs. Turn into a shallow, greased pan and bake in a very moderate oven (300° F. — Gas Mark 2) for 25 minutes.

Make the meringue: beat egg whites until stiff and dry. Gradually beat in sugar until mixture stands in peaks. Pile on to pudding and brown lightly in the oven or under the grill for a few moments.

Coconut pudding, Admiral's Inn style *(Antigua)*

4 servings:

4 oz. coconut meat, freshly grated, or dessicated coconut	2 eggs, separated
3 tablespoons sweetened condensed milk	few drops vanilla
	grated nutmeg to taste

Blend coconut, condensed milk, lightly beaten egg yolks, vanilla and nutmeg thoroughly. Turn into a greased baking dish and bake in a very moderate oven (350°F. — Gas Mark 3) until top is lightly browned. Remove from oven and cool. Beat egg whites until stiff, spread over pudding and replace in oven until golden brown.

The Admiral's Inn stands in Nelson's Dockyard at Antigua. It was the workshop in Nelson's day and had fallen into complete disrepair when the Nicholson family, father, mother and two sons sailed, with their cat, into English Harbour on their way to Australia, in 1949. They so fell in love with the dignity and beauty of the Dockyard that they went no further. They are still there today, virtually the founders of the island's prosperity.

Coconut raisin pudding *(Bahamas)*

4–6 servings:

3 eggs, lightly beaten	1 coconut, grated or 1 packet dessicated coconut
1 pint milk	8 oz. raisins, chopped
4 oz. sugar	grated nutmeg

Stir eggs, milk and sugar together, add coconut and raisins and turn into a well-greased baking tin. Sprinkle with a little nutmeg and bake in a very moderate oven (350°F. — Gas Mark 3) for 25 minutes. Serve cold.

Note:
This pudding is frequently topped with meringue, made by stiffly beating 2 egg whites with 1½ oz. sugar and browning lightly under a hot grill before chilling.

Coconut sherbet ice *(Barbados)*

4–6 servings:

10 oz. sugar
3 tablespoons water
1 pint coconut cream
  (see page 42)

2 or 3 drops almond
  essence
1½ oz. flaked coconut,
  fresh or dessicated

Cook sugar in water until completely dissolved. Allow to cool and then stir into coconut cream. Add almond essence and turn into freezing tray. Freeze, set at coldest, until the sides are mushy. Turn into a bowl and beat until frothy with an electric mixer or rotary whisk. Return to tray and freeze until firm. Garnish with a generous sprinkling of coconut.

Coffee cheese dessert *(Bahamas)*

4–6 servings:

2 teaspoons gelatine
2 tablespoons cold black
  coffee
¼ pint strong black
  coffee, very hot
2 teaspoons sugar

pinch salt
6 oz. cream cheese
2 egg whites, stiffly
  beaten
4 ripe pears
whipped cream

Soak gelatine with cold coffee for about 5 minutes. Add hot coffee, sugar and salt and stir until gelatine is completely dissolved. Beat cheese and egg whites until mixture is soft. Fold into gelatine mixture, a little at a time. Chill.

Peel, core and slice pears. When coffee cheese has been unmoulded, arrange pears around it. Serve with cream.

Coffee jelly

4 servings:

1 lb. white marshmallows	1 egg white
¾ pint strong black coffee, hot	whipped cream

Stir the marshmallows and coffee together in a double pan and heat, stirring all the time, until marshmallows are dissolved. Pour into a dish and, when jelly is on the point of setting, whisk in stiffly beaten egg white. Turn into a prepared mould, individual dishes or glasses. Serve topped with whipped cream.

Note:

Coffee jelly makes an excellent garnish for other sweets when made in a shallow square dish and chopped into squares. Try it with coffee mousse (see below).

Coffee mousse

4 servings:

1 oz. cornflour	6 tablespoons strong black coffee
4 oz. castor sugar	2 eggs, separated
pinch salt	whipped cream
2 tablespoons milk	glacé cherries, chopped

Mix cornflour, sugar and salt and beat in milk. Put over a low heat and continue beating until thickened. Remove from heat, stir in coffee, a little at a time. Return to heat and cook, stirring, for 3 minutes. Remove from heat and immediately whisk in egg yolks. Allow to cool and when it is on the point of setting, fold in lightly beaten egg whites.

Pour into individual glass dishes, cover with whipped cream and decorate with glacé cherries.

Note:

An excellent garnish is coffee jelly (above) cut in squares.

Company pie *(Jamaica)*

4–6 servings:

1 small packet corn flakes	*For the filling:*
2 oz. butter, warmed	2 bananas
3 dessertspoons honey, clear and runny	2 egg whites
	pinch salt

Crush corn flakes and mix to a paste with butter and 3 teaspoons honey. Line a shallow pie plate with mixture.
Make the filling: peel, mash and sieve bananas. Mix in unbeaten egg whites, salt and remaining honey, beat to froth like a meringue. Pile into cornflake crust. Bake for 12 minutes in a moderate oven (375°F. — Gas Mark 4).
Serve topped with coconut cream (see page 42), whipped cream or whipped cream cheese.

Coupe Nassau Royale *(Bahamas)*

4 servings:

4 fresh pineapple rings	vanilla ice cream
4 fresh peaches, stoned and thinly sliced	Nassau Royale liqueur

Arrange fruit in individual glasses, top with ice cream and flavour with a generous dash of liqueur before serving.

Nassau Royale has a slight cacao flavour. It is made, very secretly, in a cave on Grand Bahama. The story is that, towards the end of the 17th century, a French galleon was wrecked and plundered off the coast of New Providence. Among the personal goods brought into Nassau in sea chests by the pirates was a recipe for a liqueur. Many years later the manuscript came to light and with some modifications, the manufacture of Nassau Royale began, using the basis of the original French recipe. If this liqueur is unobtainable, try Jamaican Tia Maria, which has a coffee flavour.

Crêpes Nassau Royale *(Bahamas)*

4-7 servings

8 oz. flour	1 tablespoon thick cream
3½ oz. castor sugar	2 tablespoons Nassau
pinch salt	Royale liqueur,
4 eggs	rum or Tia Maria
2 egg yolks	½ oz. butter, melted
2-3 drops vanilla essence	oil for frying
¾ pint milk	castor sugar for dusting

Sift flour, stir in sugar and salt and make a well in the centre. Break in eggs and drop in extra yolks singly, drawing flour and sugar from the edges to blend thoroughly.

Work batter with a wooden spoon and add essence. Gradually stir in milk, cream and liqueur, mixing well. Heat butter until lightly browned and beat into batter. Allow to stand for 1 hour before cooking.

Heat a little oil in an omelette pan, stir batter and pour in just enough to cover the bottom of the pan. Cook lightly, shaking pan, turn and lightly brown the other side. Keep hot while remaining batter is used. Dust with castor sugar before serving, folded.

Note:

A little warm liqueur may be poured over the crêpes.

Grapefruit Alaska *(Bermuda)*

6 servings:

3 grapefruit	2 egg whites
16 marshmallows	pinch salt
4 teaspoons lemon or	1½ oz. castor sugar
lime juice	vanilla ice cream

Halve grapefruit, remove pulp and flesh. Cut away all membranes so shells are clean. Sprinkle flesh with sugar to taste, then return to shells. Chill thoroughly. Meanwhile, melt marshmallows with lemon or lime juice in a double boiler, stirring constantly, until smooth. Allow to cool. Beat egg whites and salt until forming soft peaks, then beat in remaining sugar gradually. Continue beating until very stiff. Fold in lukewarm marshmallow.

Fill each grapefruit shell with ice cream, frozen very hard, cover with meringue to seal. Bake in a very hot, pre-heated oven (500° F. — Gas Mark 9) until lightly brown, or cook for 1 minute under a hot grill. Serve immediately.

Grapefruit and melon salad *(Trinidad)*

4 servings:

1 grapefruit	honey or brown sugar
1 small melon	2–3 tablespoons Madeira or sweet sherry

Halve grapefruit and remove flesh, discarding pith and membranes. Halve melon and scoop out flesh, taking care not to damage the shell. Discard melon seeds and chop the flesh. Mix with grapefruit and sweeten to taste with honey or brown sugar. Stir in wine and stand for 1 hour before chilling. Serve in melon shells.

Grapefruit and orange flan

4–6 servings:

5 oz. sugar	1 teaspoon butter
1 oz. flour	2 large grapefruits
1 tablespoon lemon or lime juice	2 large oranges
1 egg	1 7-inch flan case, baked blind (see page 160)

Mix sugar, flour, lemon or lime juice, egg and butter with juice of 1 grapefruit. Beat thoroughly until smooth and, stirring occasionally, cook in a double boiler for 20 minutes. Peel remaining fruit removing all pith. Divide into sections. Arrange in flan case and cover with cooled sauce. Serve cold.

Grapefruit fritters *(British Virgin Islands)*

4 servings:

3½ oz. flour
1 oz. castor sugar
milk

2 large grapefruit
deep fat for frying
castor sugar for dusting

Sift flour, stir in sugar and mix to a fairly stiff batter by gradually adding milk, beating between each addition. Stand for 1 hour.

Peel grapefruit, remove all pith and cut into rings. Heat fat, dip rings in batter and fry quickly until golden brown. Drain on absorbent paper and sprinkle with castor sugar before serving on hot dishes.

Note:

These, unsweetened, are delicious with gammon or pork sausages.

Grapefruit mousse *(Jamaica)*

4 servings:

2 eggs, separated
4 oz. castor sugar
1 grapefruit or any
  citrus fruit
¼ oz. gelatine, soaked
  and melted
1 gill cream

To decorate:
chopped roasted
almonds

cherries
angelica

Cream yolks and sugar, beat in grated rind and strained grapefruit juice. Beat over a bowl of hot water until peaks form. Remove from heat and whisk until cold. Add gelatine. Beat cream lightly and mix with stiffly beaten egg whites. Fold into grapefruit mixture very gently and turn into a prepared 6-inch soufflé dish with a band of greaseproof paper extending 2 inches above the rim. Stand in a cool place until set. Decorate just before serving.

Great House torte *(Jamaica)*

6–8 servings:

1 coconut, or 1 packet of
  dessicated coconut
1¼ lbs. sweet potatoes
12 oz. brown sugar
¼ teaspoon cinnamon
¼ teaspoon grated nutmeg

¼ teaspoon allspice
2 oz. seedless raisins
2 teaspoons butter,
  melted
whipped cream

Grate coconut and squeeze through muslin, adding water a little at a time until there is 1 pint thin coconut cream (see page 42) for making with dessicated coconut. Peel and grate sweet potatoes. Stir sugar, cinnamon, nutmeg, allspice and raisins into coconut cream, then sweet potato. Mix thoroughly, stir in melted butter.

Pour mixture, which should be fairly liquid, into a well greased baking dish and bake in a moderately hot oven (400° F. — Gas Mark 5) until set and browned through, about 45 minutes.

Serve topped with whipped cream.

This recipe is a favourite of Mrs. Tenison, chatelaine of 'Good Hope', the riding ranch in the hills above Falmouth on the North Coast of Jamaica. Every big house in the islands is called a Great House, but this, to my mind, is one of the most gracious in the West Indies.

Eat your torte, served by Fred, the family butler, stroll on to the lawn with the old Weighing House building in the moonlight, the pool beyond, drink in the scent of a thousand night-blooming flowers, listen to the field hands singing their calypso accompanied by whistling frogs (that night sound of the islands which becomes an almost necessary background to your sleep). This is something you will always remember, even if you do not attempt the Great House torte when you get home.

'Good Hope' receives guests during the winter, but in summer reverts to being a private house.

Key Lime Pie *(Bahamas)*

4–6 servings:

4 eggs, separated
16 oz. condensed milk
5 oz. fresh lime juice, or
  lemon juice

1 pie shell, baked blind
  (see page 160)
4 oz. sugar

Beat yolks until light and gradually beat in condensed milk and fruit juice. Continue beating for a further 2 minutes before turning into pie shell. Beat whites with sugar until very stiff. Pile into pie and place under a hot grill until lightly browned. Chill before serving.

Latterday saints *(Trinidad)*

4 servings:

2 grapefruit
pulp of 2 oranges

$\frac{1}{2}$ oz. butter
2 oz. brown sugar

Halve grapefruit, remove pulp and mix with orange pulp. Refill grapefruit shells and top each with brown sugar and butter. Put under a slow grill and heat through till the fruit sizzles.

Mango fool

4–6 servings:

6 mangoes, full but not
  ripe
4 oz. sugar
$\frac{1}{4}$ pint water

$\frac{1}{4}$ pint milk
1 egg
3 tablespoons cream

Peel and chop mangoes. Simmer with sugar and water until soft and pulpy. Sieve or beat thoroughly. Heat milk and pour into lightly beaten egg, stirring. Return to heat and stir constantly until custard thickens. Do not allow to boil.

Cool and stir in mangoes and cream. Pour into glasses and chill.

Note:

Mashed bananas or stewed guavas may be substituted for mangoes.

In the season, round about May to June, mangoes are so plentiful in Jamaica, that every housewife tries to think of new uses and recipes, rather like plum time in England. Mangoes drop from the trees — sometimes quite disasterous if you have on a white dress; they float in the swimming pool of a house where I stay, skins of peachlike delicacy in the early morning light, flaming to brilliant orange in the setting sun. When I found a stall in Portobello Road, London, (the famous Saturday market where fruit is sold alongside silver, glass and antiques,) piled high with mangoes, in a second I was transported to Jamaica, under the big tree in the garden.

Mango ice-cream *(Jamaica)*

8–10 servings:

½ pint fresh mango pulp	4 oz. sugar
1 pint milk	1 egg
1 14-oz. can evaporated milk	few drops fresh lime or lemon juice

Sieve mango pulp and chill. Warm milk, evaporated milk and sugar until the latter dissolves. Stir into lightly beaten egg and return to heat until custard thickens. Do not allow to boil. Cool, then stir in the mango and lime juice, blending thoroughly and beating. Turn into freezer tray and freeze to a mush. Beat again and return to freezing compartment, set at coldest.

Note:

If mangoes are unobtainable, use passion fruit or ripe peaches.

Melon basket with port as made at the Montagu Beach Hotel, Nassau *(Bahamas)*

6–8 servings:

4 tablespoons port
1 large melon
½ pint whipped cream

canned cherries to
decorate

Cut a piece from the top of the melon so the fruit is the shape of a basket. Carefully scoop flesh out in small balls and soak them in the port for at least 3 hours. Add cream and turn ingredients into the basket. Serve very cold, decorated with cherries.

Matrimony *(Jamaica)*

4 servings:

4 star-apples
3 oranges
¼ pint thick cream

sugar to taste
dash of sherry (optional)

Scoop pulp out of star-apples and throw away the pips. Slice oranges, peeled and with pips and pith removed, blend with star-apple pulp. Add the cream, beaten and sweetened to taste (or substitute sweetened condensed milk, adding no extra sugar). Blend all ingredients well, add sherry, pour into individual glasses and chill before serving.

Some Jamaicans do not use cream in Matrimony and often blend star-apples and oranges. Although this dessert cannot be made without star-apples, it cannot be left out of this book. Star-apples are a fairly large fruit, which when cut open, have a star in the centre, with the pips all around and are rather tasteless without other fruit.

Orange and ginger salad

4 servings:

4 large oranges
4 pieces preserved ginger, chopped finely

For decoration:
1 small ripe banana
lemon juice or lime juice

2 tablespoons preserved ginger syrup
1 tablespoon curaçao or cherry brandy

maraschino cherries
whipped cream

Peel and divide oranges into sections. Chop sections into small pieces and stir in ginger, syrup and liqueur. Mix thoroughly and stand for 2 hours.
Slice banana and sprinkle with lime or lemon juice. Divide orange and ginger mixture between serving dishes and decorate with banana, cherries and cream.

Oranges baked

4 servings:

4 oranges
boiling water
4 generous teaspoons butter

2 oz. brown sugar
$\frac{1}{2}$ oz. castor sugar
thick cream

Wash oranges and cover with water. Cook gently until skins are tender, drain and neatly slice tops off. Pull cores out and place the oranges in a casserole. Push 1 teaspoon butter and 1 tablespoon brown sugar in the centre of each orange, cap with the tops and sprinkle with castor sugar. Pour $\frac{1}{2}$ inch of water into the bottom of the dish, cover and bake in a very moderate oven (350°F. — Gas Mark 3) for 20 minutes. Remove lid and continue baking for 10 minutes until castor sugar forms a golden crust. Serve hot with cream.

Note:
Delicious with meat or poultry, using less sugar.

Orange custard cups (*Jamaica*)

4–6 servings:

1 sweet Seville orange	1 pint cream or rich milk
1 tablespoon brandy	preserved orange for
4 oz. loaf sugar	decoration
egg yolks	(see page 217)

Squeeze juice from orange and set aside. Boil half the orange rind in a little water until tender. Beat in a mortar until fine, then stir in brandy, orange juice, sugar and egg yolks. Stir thoroughly. Bring the cream or milk to the boil and stir slowly into mixture. Beat until cold. Turn into individual custard cups and stand in a large dish of hot water until set. Stick a small sliver of candied orange peel into each and eat hot or chilled.

This recipe is taken from the collection of old family recipes that is to be published by the Jamaica Tourist Board. Preserved citrus is a speciality of Jamaica.

Orange fritters

4 servings:

3½ oz. flour	milk
1 oz. castor sugar	2 large oranges
deep fat for frying	castor sugar for dusting

Sift flour, stir in sugar and mix to a fairly stiff batter by gradually adding milk. Beat well between each addition. Allow batter to stand for 1 hour.
Peel oranges and divide into sections removing all loose skin. Heat fat until smoke rises, dip orange pieces into batter, then fry until golden brown. Drain on absorbent paper and dust with sugar. Serve immediately.

Orange soufflé with citrus sauce

4 servings:

4 eggs
5 oz. sugar
juice and grated rind of
  1 orange

For the sauce:
finely grated rind and
  juice of 1 orange
½ pint water
2 teaspoons cornflour

Separate eggs and beat yolks until thick and orange-coloured. Gradually beat in 2½ oz. sugar, add orange juice and rind. Beat egg whites and gradually beat in remaining sugar. Fold into yolk mixture and bake for 40 minutes in a very moderate oven (300° F. — Gas Mark 2).

Make the sauce: simmer orange rind in water for 10 minutes. Mix cornflour with a little cold water, add to orange rind water, then add orange juice. Stir and simmer for 3 minutes. Serve separately.

Orange surprise *(Bahamas)*

4–6 servings:

3 eggs
½ pint milk
4 oz. sugar
3 oranges, peeled and
  thinly sliced

For the topping:
2 egg whites
4 oz. sugar
pinch salt

Beat eggs lightly, then pour milk, heated with sugar, over. Stir thoroughly and cook gently in a double boiler until thickened. Line a dish with orange slices, keeping a slice for decoration. Allow to cool, then put in the refrigerator for 3 hours.

Make the topping: whisk whites stiffly and gradually beat in sugar and salt, beating until mixture stands in peaks.

Scoop on to chilled pudding, brown lightly for a few seconds under a hot grill and serve cold, decorated with orange.

Orange whip

4 servings:

3 eggs, separated	2 tablespoons hot water
5 oz. castor sugar	2 teaspoons powdered
finely grated rind of	gelatine, soaked in 1
1 orange	tablespoon cold water
7 tablespoons fresh orange	whipped cream
juice	

Beat yolks with sugar until light and creamy. Stir in orange rind and juice. Pour water on to gelatine and stir until dissolved. Add to egg mixture and stir thoroughly. Whip whites until stiff and fold into orange mixture. Turn into a bowl or individual dishes to set.

Pancake mix, Chef Anthony style *(Bahamas)*

8 oz. flour	4 eggs
3 oz. castor sugar	2 tablespoons brandy
1 pint milk	(optional)

Mix all ingredients together and whip until very smooth, when the batter is ready for use.

Fruit pancake

Pour a thin layer of pancake mix (see above) in a lightly buttered pan, sprinkle on some chopped peaches or other fruit, cover with another layer of mixture and fry on both sides in butter. Sprinkle with icing sugar and serve very hot.

Pancakes

4 servings:

4 oz. plain flour	$\frac{1}{2}$ pint milk
pinch salt	castor sugar
2 eggs	oil for frying

Sieve flour and salt and make a well in the centre. Drop eggs in and a little milk. Stir, drawing in the flour from the sides, and beat until smooth. Add milk a little at a time, stirring and beating between each addition. Pour batter into a jug and stand in a cool place for at least 1 hour. Just before using, beat the batter again.

In a 7-inch pan, heat 1 teaspoon oil and shake pan so that it is greased all over. Pour off any excess and quickly pour in sufficient batter to cover the bottom of the pan thinly. Turn pan about over the heat so that batter cooks quickly and evenly. When underside is nicely browned, turn or toss the pancake and cook lightly on the other side.

Turn each pancake on to a warmed plate as it is cooked and keep warm. Sprinkle with castor sugar or a filling and serve.

Note:
This quantity makes 8 7-inch pancakes.

Peachy cream *(Bahamas)*

4–6 servings:

2 cans condensed milk	
2 pints water	1 20-oz. can peaches
3 eggs	2 oz. sugar

Stir milk and water together. Beat eggs until pale and thick and mash drained peaches thoroughly. Add eggs and peaches to milk mixture and stir in peach syrup and sugar. Turn into a freezing tray and freeze in the icing compartment, set at coldest. Stir occasionally as the sweet hardens.

Peanut cream *(Bahamas)*

6–8 servings:

4 oz. fresh peanuts	½ pint cream
rind of 1 lemon or 2 limes	1½ oz. icing sugar
¼ pint water	1 oz. gelatine, dissolved
½ pint milk	in 1 tablespoon water

Pound peanuts to make a flour, stir in lemon or lime rind, finely grated, add water slowly and mix to a stiff paste. Heat milk, cream and icing sugar, stirring. Mix in gelatine and strain. Return to heat, stir in peanut paste and bring to the boil. Cook, stirring, for 2 minutes. Cool and turn into a mould. Chill before serving.

Pekin dust No. 1 *(Netherlands Antilles)*

6–8 servings:

1½ pounds chestnuts	2 oz. sugar
½ teaspoon powdered ginger	4 tablespoons thick cream
¼ teaspoon salt	

To decorate:

preserved kumquats	chopped nuts
orange slices	

Cross-slit chestnuts on top and drop into boiling water. Cook until shells burst and nuts are soft. Drain, allow to cool, then peel. Force through a food mill or pound to a pulp. Stir in ginger, salt and sugar, mixing well.
Beat cream until thick and fold into chestnut mixture. Press into a greased mould or greased individual moulds. Turn out and decorate.

Pekin dust No. 2

4 oz. sugar	squeeze lemon or lime
¼ pint water	juice

Boil the sugar and water until golden brown. Add lemon or lime juice and pour into buttered cake tin to set. Cover with a clean cloth and crush with a rolling pin till it is about the consistency of coffee sugar. Serve with sliced oranges or bananas.

Pineapple baked *(Barbados)*

4–6 servings:

1 medium-sized pineapple	1 teaspoon powdered
2 oz. sugar	cinnamon
4 tablespoons rum	

With a curved knife (the kind used for preparing grapefruit) scoop out pineapple flesh without piercing the shell. Discard all pith and dice flesh, catching any juice. Thoroughly coat fruit in sugar, turn into the shell and pour over any juice and 2 tablespoons rum. Top with a sprinkling of cinnamon.
Skewer pineapple top in position with cocktail sticks and bake in a moderate oven (375° F. — Gas Mark 4) for 20–30 minutes, or until tender. Remove skewers, heat remaining rum and pour over the entire pineapple. Set alight and serve flaming.

Pineapple milk sherbet

6–8 servings:

6 tablespoons pineapple, chopped	juice of ½ orange
	1 pint milk
juice of 1 fresh lime, or lemon	8 oz. sugar

Set aside a few pieces of the pineapple for decoration and mix remainder with fruit juice and chill. Warm milk enough to dissolve the sugar, then chill. When both pineapple and milk are thoroughly cold, beat together, turn into a freezing tray and freeze until mushy. Remove, beat again and return to the freezer, set at coldest.

Pineapple pancakes

4 servings:

basic pancake batter
(see page 179)

For the filling:
3 tablespoons fresh or
  tinned pineapple
2 tablespoons strawberry
  jam

grated rind and juice of
  ½ lemon or 1 lime

Chop pineapple finely and heat with jam, rind and juice, stirring thoroughly. Spread each pancake with filling, roll up and serve.

Pineapple pie *(Bahamas)*

4–6 servings:

1 20-oz. can crushed
  pineapple
8 oz. granulated sugar
4 oz. glucose
1½ oz. cornflour

juice and grated rind of
  half a lemon or 1 lime
short pastry to line and
  cover an 8-inch pie
  plate (see page 160)
1 white of egg

Mix pineapple, sugar, glucose, cornflour and lime or lemon and turn into a greased pie plate, lined with short pastry. Cover with pastry, glaze with white of egg. Bake in a moderately hot oven (400° F. — Gas Mark 5) for 25–30 minutes.

Pineapple supreme, Chef Anthony style *(Bahamas)*

6–8 servings:

1 large pineapple
2 oranges
1 grapefruit

4 tablespoons Kirsch
4 oz. cream
2 oz. castor sugar

Cut top off pineapple and scoop flesh out. Cut in half and put half aside for another meal. Dice remaining half. Peel oranges and grapefruit, removing all pith, and cut into segments. Add to pineapple, cream, Kirsch and sugar. Pack into pineapple shell and serve very cold.

Rum apples

4 servings:

4 cooking apples of even size	1 drop vanilla essence if liked
3 oz. sugar	4 tablespoons rum
$\frac{1}{3}$ pint water	

Peel and core apples without breaking them. Arrange in a shallow, flameproof dish. Stir sugar into water, add vanilla and pour over apples. Cover and poach very gently until soft but still whole. Lift the apples out carefully with a pierced spoon to drain off liquid. Keep hot in the oven.
Reduce syrup until thick. Stir in $2\frac{1}{2}$ tablespoons rum and pour over apples. Just before serving, heat remaining rum, set light and pour over apples.

Rum ice cream *(Jamaica)*

6–8 servings:

3 eggs	$\frac{1}{2}$ pint cream
2 oz. sugar	2 tablespoons dark rum
1 pint milk	

Beat eggs lightly, add sugar and stir in warmed milk. Cook in a double boiler, stirring, until custard thickens. Allow to cool. Stir in cream and rum, blending thoroughly. Beat well, turn into freezing tray and freeze to a mush. Remove, beat, then return to freezer, set at coldest.

Note:
This is very good with sherry or marsala instead of rum.

Rum pancakes *(Barbados)*

4–6 servings:

5 oz. plain flour	*For the filling:*
1 teaspoon sugar	½ pint thick cream
1 egg	2 tablespoons rum
1 egg yolk	2 teaspoons castor sugar
1 tablespoon olive oil	
1 tablespoon rum	*To garnish:*
½ pint milk	grated chocolate
olive or nut oil for frying	

Sift flour, stir in sugar, egg and egg yolk, oil and rum. Blend thoroughly. Beat in milk, a little at a time until batter is smooth and the consistency of thin cream. Add a little more milk if necessary. Stand for 1 hour.

Prepare the filling: whip cream until thick. Stir in rum and sugar and keep bowl over warm water.

Brush omelette pan with oil, fry thin pancakes. Keep warm in a cool oven. When all are cooked, quickly spread with filling, roll up, sprinkle with chocolate and serve hot.

Rum syllabub *(Bequia)*

4 servings:

2 oz. castor sugar	juice of 1 small lemon
½ pint cream	or 2 limes
	3 tablespoons rum

Whip all ingredients in a large bowl until quite stiff. Carefully spoon mixture into tall glasses and leave for 8 hours in a cool place to set.

By then there should be a little rum at the bottom of each glass and the cream should be nicely firm on top.

Steamed raisin pudding *(Grenada)*

6–8 servings:

1½ oz. butter
3 oz. sugar
3 eggs, lightly beaten
8 oz. flour
¼ teaspoon cinnamon
¼ teaspoon grated nutmeg

½ teaspoon bicarbonate
  of soda
8 tablespoons sour milk
10 oz. raisins, chopped
  and dredged in flour

Beat butter and sugar until creamy, beat in eggs a little at a time. Sift flour, cinnamon, nutmeg and soda and add to mixture, a little at a time, alternately with milk. Blend thoroughly. Stir in raisins, turn into a greased pudding basin and steam gently for 3 hours.

Steamed West India pudding

4–6 servings:

4 oz. plain flour
½ teaspoon bicarbonate of
  soda
1½ oz. lard
1½ oz. brown sugar
¼ teaspoon mixed spice

4 oz. West India treacle,
  warmed
1 egg, lightly beaten
3 tablespoons sour milk,
  or fresh milk mixed
  with 1 teaspoon vinegar

Sift flour with bicarbonate of soda and rub in lard. Stir in sugar, spice, treacle, egg and milk. Mix thoroughly and turn into a greased basin. Steam for 1½ hours.

Note:

The pudding mixture can be prepared in advance, if necessary the day before. Before steaming, stir briskly and turn into the basin.

Sweet potato and coconut pudding *(Barbados)*

6–8 servings:

2 lb. sweet potatoes	1 lb. sugar
2 coconuts, grated or 1	grated rind and juice
packet dessicated coconut	of 1 lemon or 2 limes

Peel, boil and mash potatoes. Blend with remaining ingredients, turn into a large, shallow well- greased baking pan. Bake in a very moderate oven (350° F. — Gas Mark 3) for about 1 hour.

Sweet potato pudding *(Nevis)*

4–6 servings:

2 oz. sweet potato, peeled	2 oz. currants
and grated	2 oz. raisins
8 oz. sugar	2 oz. butter, melted
½ pint coconut cream	1 teaspoon mixed spice
(see page 42)	½ teaspoon powdered
	ginger

Blend all ingredients thoroughly and turn into a buttered baking dish. Cook for 1 hour in a very moderate oven (350° F. — Gas Mark 3) and serve hot.
Extra coconut cream may be poured over each serving.

Sweet potato puff *(St. Kitts)*

6–8 servings:

4 sweet potatoes	1 oz. butter
1 teaspoon salt	2 oz. flaked or dessicated
4 tablespoons sugar	coconut
¾ pint coconut cream	
(see page 42)	

Boil potatoes in their skins until tender. Peel and mash

186

smoothly. Stir in salt, sugar and coconut cream and beat together thoroughly. Turn mixture into a buttered 9-inch pie plate and bake for 20 minutes in a moderately hot oven (400° F. — Gas Mark 5) when the puff should be lightly browned. Fry coconut in butter until light brown and sprinkle on top of the puff.

This dish may be served hot or cold.

Tropical delight pudding

4 servings:

4 bananas	1½ oz. grated coconut or
juice of 1 orange	dessicated coconut
2 oz. brown sugar	

Halve peeled bananas lengthways and arrange in a greased pie dish. Stir orange juice into sugar and spread over bananas. Sprinkle thickly with coconut and bake in a moderately hot oven (400° F. — Gas Mark 5), until fruit is soft and coconut browned.

Tropical duff pudding *(New Providence)*

6–8 servings:

4 oz. butter	12 oz. flour
6 oz. sugar	6 teaspoons baking
4 eggs	powder
1 coconut, grated or 1	milk and water to mix
packet dessicated coconut	

Beat butter and sugar until creamy, then beat in eggs, one at a time. Sift coconut, flour and baking powder and stir in. Mix to a stiff dough with milk and water, turn into a greased basin, cover with greaseproof and muslin and steam for 2 hours.

Note:

Left-overs can be fried lightly in butter.

Tropical oranges

6 servings:

6 oranges	6 teaspoons brown sugar
9 dates, pitted	6 teaspoons Cointreau
8 dried figs	(optional)
6 marshmallows	1½ tablespoons rum
1 tablespoon unsalted	
almonds or cashews,	
finely chopped	

Wash oranges, slice tops off at the stalk ends and remove pulp. Discard skin and pips and mix with chopped dates, figs, marshmallows and nuts. Press into orange shells and add 1 teaspoon brown sugar to each. Skewer orange tops on and bake for 30 minutes in a moderate oven (375°F. — Gas Mark 4).
Remove caps, add 1 teaspoon Cointreau to each orange and arrange in a serving dish. Heat rum, pour over oranges and serve flaming.

West Indian fruit pie *(British Virgin Islands)*

6 servings:

4 tablespoons fresh	¼ teaspoon salt
pineapple, cubed	½ oz. flour
2 fresh pears, peeled,	juice and grated rind
quartered and cored	of 1 lemon or 2 limes
2 bananas, cut small	short pastry to line and
4 or 5 dried figs, chopped	cover 9-inch pie plate
4 oz. brown sugar	(see page 160)

Put pineapple into a bowl, add pears, bananas and figs. Stir in sugar, salt, flour, lemon or lime. Stir all together well. Line pie plate with pastry and turn mixture in. Cover with pastry and bake for 15 minutes in a hot oven (425°F. — Gas Mark 6). Reduce heat to 350°F. — Gas Mark 3, cook for 45 minutes. Serve very hot with rum sauce (see page 43).

West Indies plum pudding *(Grenada)*

8–10 servings:

1 lb. raisins, stoned
1 lb. currants, cleaned and washed
8 oz. peel, chopped
½ pint rum
1 lb. stale bread
1 pint milk
8 oz. brown sugar

6 eggs
1 lb. beef suet, finely chopped
¼ pint wine
¼ pint brandy
1 tablespoon mixed and powdered nutmeg, mace, cinnamon and cloves

Mix raisins, currants and peel, put into jars, cover with rum and keep for at least 1 week before use.

Soak bread in warmed milk, add sugar, eggs, prepared fruit, suet, wine, brandy and spices. Beat together, add whites eggs. Turn into a greased pudding basin, cover and steam for 6 hours.

Turn on to a warmed dish, pour over a little more brandy and serve alight in the traditional way.

Wine jelly *(Nassau)*

4–6 servings:

1 oz. gelatine
¾ pint water
8 oz. sugar
8 tablespoons sherry, or any wine to taste

3 tablespoons fresh orange juice
3 tablespoons fresh lemon or lime juice

Soak gelatine in 2 tablespoons water for about 5 minutes. Bring remaining water to boiling point, stir in soaked gelatine and stir until dissolved. Add remaining ingredients, stir thoroughly and strain into a wet mould. Allow to set and chill before serving.

Yoghurt ice-cream *(British Virgin Islands)*

4 servings:

2 cartons plain yoghurt	4 oz. ground nuts,
2 eggs	almonds or cashew nuts
4 tablespoons honey	12 plumped seedless
¼ pint milk	raisins
¼ pint strong black coffee	pinch salt

Scald milk, add honey, eggs and salt very slowly, then the coffee. Cook for 1 minute in a double saucepan, until it begins to thicken; add nuts and raisins, fold in yoghurt. Allow to cool, stirring from time to time.

Pour into the ice tray, put in the refrigerator, set at cold until the sides of tray begin to freeze. Take out and stir, return to freezing compartment. Repeat the stirring process once more, then freeze for 2 hours.

This is sometimes made with small pieces of preserved ginger instead of nuts and raisins or it can be made entirely of yoghurt, sweetened with honey and given body with either nuts and raisins or ginger. The above method, however, gives a richer, smoother ice cream. Although I did not have this in the West Indies, I have made yoghurt ice with crumbled brown bread to give it body and honey as a sweetener.

Cakes, cookies and biscuits

Teatime is usually observed in the islands and most West Indians have a sweet tooth and a liking for rich cakes.

Bananas again figure in many recipes, banana bread is found in varying forms right through the islands. Recipes from Grenada, the 'Spice Island', nearly always use nutmeg which grows in quantities on the island. Nutmeg comes from the dried kernel of the Myristica fragrans, an evergreen tree bearing a small fruit like a red berry. On sale in Grenada are little nutmeg mills, a cross between a coffee grinder and a pepper mill. Cassava is also used for bread and biscuits in the West Indies but it is not found in all parts of the world, so I have included only one of these recipes. Oranges and lemons, pineapple and rum appear again at tea time. Treacle is a favourite sweetener and coconut is very popular.

Baked sugar doughnuts *(Bermuda)*

2¼ lb. flour
1 teaspoon salt
1½ teaspoons baking
  powder
grated rind of ½ lemon
1¾ lb. vegetable
  shortening
1 egg

3 tablespoons evaporated
  milk

For the syrup:
12 oz. sugar

4 tablespoons water
pink colouring

Sift flour, salt and baking powder, stir in lemon rind and rub in shortening. Make a well in the centre and drop in the eggs and evaporated milk, blending thoroughly. Turn on to a floured board and roll until ½ inch thick. Use a doughnut cutter or cut strips, joining the ends to make doughnut rings. Bake on a greased baking sheet for 15 minutes in a hot oven (400° F. — Gas mark 5).

Make the syrup: stir sugar and water in a saucepan, bring to the boil and boil until a thick syrup. Add colouring, pour over cold doughnuts, turning them until the syrup is absorbed.

Note:

These doughnuts will keep in airtight tins for 3–4 months.

Banana biscuits *(Jamaica)*

2 oz. butter
3 oz. castor sugar
1 egg yolk
7 oz. flour
2 oz. cornflour

pinch salt
½ teaspoon vanilla
  essence
2 bananas, well mashed

Cream butter and sugar until light and fluffy and beat in egg yolk. Sift flour cornflour and salt and stir into creamed mixture. Add vanilla essence and bananas and blend thoroughly. Turn on to a floured board and roll out thinly. Cut into strips, arrange on a greased baking sheet and bake for 15 minutes in a moderate oven (375° F. — Gas Mark 4). Cool on a wire rack before storing.

Banana bread *(Jamaica)*

4 oz. butter	8 oz. flour
8 oz. castor sugar	1 teaspoon bicarbonate
2 eggs, lightly beaten	of soda
3 bananas, thoroughly	1 teaspoon salt
mashed	2 oz. walnuts, chopped

Cream butter and sugar well then gradually stir in lightly beaten eggs, then bananas. Sift flour and bicarbonate of soda and stir into mixture, a little at a time, until well blended. Mix in nuts and turn into a greased 8 inch x 4 inch loaf tin. Bake for 1 hour in a very moderate oven (350°F. — Gas Mark 3).

Note:

There are infinite varieties of banana bread and most Caribbean cooks have their own favourites. Some do not include nuts, others have less egg and add a little sour milk. All kinds are served hot or cold, sliced and buttered.

Banana layer cake *(Bahamas)*

9 oz. flour	4 oz. butter, warmed
1 teaspoon baking powder	
$\frac{1}{2}$ teaspoon bicarbonate	*For the filling:*
of soda	whipped cream
pinch salt	2 teaspoons castor sugar
10 oz. castor sugar	1 banana, chopped
5 bananas, well mashed	
2 eggs	

Sift together flour, baking powder, soda and salt and stir sugar in. Make a well in the centre and drop in 2 tablespoons banana with eggs and warmed butter. Beat thoroughly. Add remaining banana and beat again, for at least 3 minutes. Turn mixture into 2 greased 8-inch sandwich tins and bake for 25 minutes in a moderately hot oven (375°F. — Gas Mark 4). Turn on to a cake rack to cool.
Whisk cream and sugar, stir in banana and sandwich the cakes.

Banana muffins *(Bahamas)*

6½ oz. flour	½ teaspoon salt
1 tablespoon cornflour	2 oz. butter
1 teaspoon baking powder	3 oz. castor sugar
½ teaspoon bicarbonate of soda	1 egg
	3 bananas, well mashed

Sift flour, cornflour, baking powder, soda and salt. Cream butter and sugar until light and soft. Beat egg lightly and beat into the creamed mixture. Add flour mixture and mashed bananas alternately, a little at a time, mixing thoroughly but not beating. Bake in well-greased, deep patty tins in a moderately hot oven (400° F. — Gas Mark 5) for 20 minutes. Serve hot or cold, with or without butter.

Banana oatmeal biscuits *(Grenada)*

6 oz. flour	6 oz. butter
8 oz. sugar	1 egg, lightly beaten
½ teaspoon baking soda	3 bananas, well mashed
1 teaspoon salt	4 oz. rolled oats
¼ teaspoon grated nutmeg	2 tablespoons walnuts, chopped
¼ teaspoon ground cinnamon	

Sift flour, sugar, soda, salt, nutmeg and cinnamon together. Rub in butter. Make a well in the centre and drop in the egg and mashed bananas, mixing into the dry ingredients by drawing them into the centre. Stir in oats and chopped nuts and beat together thoroughly. Using a teaspoon, drop blobs of the mixture on to a greased baking sheet, allowing about 1 inch between them for spreading. Bake in a moderately hot oven (400° F. — Gas Mark 5) for 15 minutes, when the edges should be browned. Remove immediately with a palette knife and cool on a wire rack.

Banana oat cookies *(Bermuda)*

6 oz. flour
8 oz. sugar
1½ teaspoons baking
  powder
1 teaspoon salt
1 teaspoon powdered
  cinnamon
1 teaspoon powdered
  nutmeg

6 oz. shortening
1 egg
4 ripe bananas, mashed
4 oz. quick-cooking oats
3 tablespoons chopped
  nuts
1 teaspoon vanilla
  essence

Sift flour, stir in sugar, baking powder, salt, cinnamon and nutmeg and cut in the shortening. Beat egg with bananas and add to the mixture. Stir in oats, nuts and vanilla and beat thoroughly. Using a teaspoon, drop small mounds of the mixture on to an ungreased baking sheet, about 1 inch apart. Bake in a moderately hot oven (400° F. — Gas Mark 5) for about 15 minutes, then remove quickly from the baking sheet.

Banana yoghurt bread

4 oz. butter or margarine
8 oz. soft brown sugar
10 oz. whole wheat flour
1 teaspoon bicarbonate
  of soda

pinch salt
¼ pint yoghurt
4 large ripe bananas, well
  mashed
2 eggs, lightly beaten

Cream butter and sugar, sift flour, soda and salt, and beat together yoghurt, mashed bananas and eggs. Add a little flour and yoghurt mixtures alternately to the butter and sugar, beating well between each addition. Turn into an oiled loaf tin and bake in a very moderate oven (350° F — Gas Mark 3) for 1 hour.

Note:
If two small loaves are made from these quantities, reduce the cooking time by 5 minutes.

Blueberry muffins *(Bahamas)*

4 oz. butter
8 oz. castor sugar
pinch salt
3 eggs
10 oz. flour

1½ teaspoons baking
powder
4 tablespoons milk
8 oz. blueberries

Cream butter, sugar and salt until light and fluffy. Add eggs, one at a time, beating each in thoroughly. Sift flour and baking powder and add to mixture, a little at a time, alternately with the milk. Lightly fold blueberries into mixture and turn into well-greased, deep patty tins. Bake in a moderately hot oven (400° F. — Gas Mark 5) for 20 minutes.

Bride's dark fruit cake *(Bermuda)*

2 lb. seedless raisins
8 oz. currants
8 oz. mixed candied peel
8 oz. candied cherries
scant ½ pint black rum
1 lb. butter
1 lb. sugar
12 small eggs, separated
1 lb. flour
½ teaspoon salt
1 teaspoon baking
powder

1½ teaspoons ground
cinnamon
1½ teaspoons allspice
½ teaspoon ground mace
½ teaspoon grated
nutmeg
8 oz. molasses
8 oz. brandy
1 lb. almonds, blanched
and halved
2 tablespoons lemon or
lime juice

Prepare and cut up the dried fruit and soak in the rum for 1 week. Cream butter and sugar until light and fluffy and beat in the beaten egg yolks. Sift flour, salt, baking powder, cinnamon, allspice, mace and nutmeg and stir brandy into molasses. Add dry ingredients and brandy mixture alternately, a little at a time, to butter mixture, blending well. Fold in beaten egg whites, almonds and lime or lemon juice. Turn into a large cake tin (9 ins. x 13 ins.), well lined with greaseproof paper and bake in a moderate oven (350° F. — Gas Mark 2) for about 2½ hours.

Cassava pie crust *(Bahamas)*

12 large sticks cassava	salt
2 oz. butter	Cayenne pepper
2 oz. lard	grated nutmeg
6 eggs, lightly beaten	

Grate the cassava and squeeze through several thicknesses of muslin to remove the water. Stir in the butter, lard, eggs. Add salt, pepper and nutmeg to taste.

Note:

This is an excellent crust for pies such as chicken pie, for which you would line a pie dish, with the crust, fill with cooked chicken and gravy, cover with crust and bake in a moderate oven (375° F. — Gas Mark 4), for about 1 hour.

Coconut macaroon biscuits *(Bahamas)*

4 oz. sugar	*For the topping:*
4 oz. butter	4 oz. coconut, grated
2 egg yolks	2 oz. cornflour
8 oz. flour	6 oz. icing sugar
pinch salt	2 egg whites

Cream sugar and butter until light, then beat in egg yolks. Sift flour and salt and work into creamed mixture to make a stiff dough. On a floured board, roll out to $\frac{1}{8}$-inch thick, cut into shapes and bake on a greased baking sheet in a hot oven (400° F. — Gas Mark 5) for 10 minutes. Allow to cool. *Make the topping:* stir together coconut, cornflour and sugar. Gradually beat in egg whites to make a stiff mixture. Spread on the biscuit bases and bake in a very slow oven (250° F. — Gas Mark $\frac{1}{2}$) for just long enough to set the macaroon topping.

Corn muffins *(Bahamas)*

4 oz. butter	8 oz. cornmeal
8 oz. castor sugar	1 pint milk
pinch salt	1 lb. cake flour
3 eggs	1 oz. baking powder

Cream butter, sugar and salt until light and fluffy. Beat in eggs one at a time, then add, alternately, the cornmeal and milk a little at a time. Sift cake flour and baking powder and lightly fold into mixture. Turn into well greased deep patty tins and bake in a moderately hot oven (400° F. — Gas Mark 5) for about 20 minutes.

Date and nut loaf *(Bahamas)*

6 oz. dates, pitted	8 oz. sugar
¼ pint boiling water	2 eggs
1 teaspoon bicarbonate of soda	3 tablespoons walnuts, broken
2 oz. butter	6 oz. flour

Chop dates finely, mix water and bicarbonate of soda and pour over dates. Leave to cool. Meanwhile, cream butter and sugar until light and fluffy, beat in eggs, one at a time, then stir in date and water mixture. Stir in walnuts. Gradually add sifted flour, beating until smooth but thin. Turn into a well-greased loaf tin and bake in a very slow oven (275° F. — Gas Mark 1) for 1¼ hours, when the bread should be dark brown and firm to the touch. Serve sliced thinly and buttered.

Note:

This bread will keep fresh for about a fortnight.

Ginger cookies *(Bermuda)*

4 oz. butter
2 oz. margarine
10 oz. brown sugar
2 eggs, lightly beaten
1 tablespoon bicarbonate
of soda

1 tablespoon hot water
4 tablespoons powdered
ginger
10 oz. flour
pinch salt

Cream fats and sugar thoroughly, beat in eggs, then bicarbonate of soda dissolved in water. Sift ginger, flour and salt and beat into the mixture, a little at a time. With a teaspoon, drop blobs of mixture, about 2 inches apart on to a greased baking tin. Bake in a very moderate oven (350° F. — Gas Mark 3) for 20 minutes, when the cookies should be lightly browned.

Grandma's famous gingerbread *(Trinidad)*

10 oz. flour
4 oz. castor sugar
pinch salt
1 teaspoon ground ginger
½ teaspoon mixed spice

½ teaspoon bicarbonate
of soda
3 oz. butter
2 eggs
4 oz. West India treacle
milk

Blend all dry ingredients together. Warm butter and work into mixture, add eggs and warmed treacle. Mix to a light batter consistency with about 4 tablespoons milk, according to the size of the eggs. Turn into a shallow, well-greased tin and bake in a moderate oven (375° F. — Gas Mark 4) for 30 minutes. Serve sliced and buttered.

Guava jelly cookies *(Bermuda)*

4 oz. butter
2 oz. granulated sugar
1 egg yolk, lightly beaten
few drops vanilla
4 oz. flour

pinch salt
1 egg white
3 tablespoons chopped nuts
3 oz. guava jelly

Cream butter and sugar and beat in egg yolk, then vanilla. Sift flour and salt and add, a little at a time, to mixture, beating thoroughly. Divide and shape with the fingers, into small balls — this quantity should make about 15. Roll each ball in egg white and then in nuts. Using a finger, make a small hole in each cookie and fill it with jelly. Bake on a greased baking sheet, jelly uppermost, for 20 minutes in a very moderate oven (350° F. — Gas Mark 3). Allow plenty of room for spreading between each cookie.

Note:

Other jelly or thick jam could be substituted for the guava jelly, but this is obtainable in Oriental shops.

Guava oatmeal squares *(Jamaica)*

8 oz. flour
4 oz. rolled oats
6 oz. brown sugar
½ teaspoon baking powder

1 teaspoon salt
6 oz. butter or margarine
guava jam (see page 220)

Sift flour and mix in oats, sugar, baking powder and salt. Cut in butter. Pack rather more than half the mixture into a greased, shallow pan, spread with jam and sprinkle remaining oatmeal mixture on top. Bake in a moderate oven (375° F. — Gas Mark 4) for about 20 minutes. Before completely cold, cut into squares.

Note:

Other jams, such as apricot or pineapple jam could be substituted for the guava jam.

Honey butter tarts *(Bermuda)*

flaky pastry (see page 118)
4 oz. butter
12 oz. honey
6 oz. brown sugar

8 oz. raisins, seedless
¼ teaspoon grated nutmeg
¼ teaspoon salt
2 eggs, lightly beaten

Thoroughly chill pastry then line 12 patty tins. Melt butter and stir in honey, sugar, raisins, nutmeg and salt. Blend thoroughly and allow to cool. Add eggs. Spoon mixture into pastry cases. Bake on the lowest rack of a hot oven (450° F. — Gas Mark 7) for 15–20 minutes. Allow to stand for at least 10 minutes before removing from tins.

Nut bread *(Bahamas)*

8 oz. flour
2 teaspoons baking
powder
4 oz. sugar
pinch salt

1 egg, lightly beaten
8 tablespoons milk
6 tablespoons dates,
chopped
4 tablespoons nuts,
chopped

Sift flour and baking powder, stir in sugar and salt. Make a well in the centre and drop egg in, then milk, dates and nuts. Mix thoroughly, cover bowl and allow to stand for 30 minutes. Bake in a greased loaf tin, in a very moderate oven (350° F. — Gas Mark 3) for about 1 hour.

Nutmeg almond cookies *(Grenada)*

12 oz. flour, sifted
12 oz. sugar
1 teaspoon baking powder
1 teaspoon ground nutmeg
8 oz. butter or margarine
1 large egg, beaten
1 tablespoon water
½ teaspoon almond essence
6 oz. walnuts or 1 oz. blanched almonds

Sift together flour, sugar, baking powder and nutmeg. Cut in butter or margarine until mixture looks like crumbs. Combine egg, water and almond essence, add to flour mixture. Mix to a stiff dough, then chill for 2 hours or until stiff enough to handle.

Shape into small balls, place on an ungreased baking sheet, flatten balls with a glass, covered with greaseproof paper. Press half a blanched almond or walnut in the centre of each. Bake in a very moderate oven (350° F. — Gas Mark 3) for 12 minutes or until cookies have browned at the edges.

Nutmeg date bars *(Grenada)*

8 oz. dates, pitted and minced or finely chopped
8 oz. pecan or walnuts, chopped
4 oz. icing sugar, sifted
2 large eggs, beaten
½ teaspoon salt
½ oz. butter, melted
1 tablespoon lemon or lime juice
1 oz. flour, sifted
¾ teaspoon nutmeg, ground
icing sugar

Mix dates and nuts with sugar, eggs and salt. Add butter, lemon or lime juice, flour and nutmeg. Blend thoroughly. Grease a square baking tin (about 2 inches deep) with butter, spread mixture in about ⅜-inch thick. Bake in a very moderate oven (325° F. — Gas Mark 3) for 30 minutes. Allow to cool, cut in bars or squares and roll in icing sugar.

Nutmeg sugar cookies *(Grenada)*

6 oz. flour
2 teaspoons baking
   powder
¼ teaspoon salt
4 oz. butter, softened
¾ teaspoon nutmeg,
   ground

8 oz. sugar
1 large egg
hundreds and thousands

Sift flour and baking powder, add salt. Set aside. Blend butter, nutmeg and sugar, beat in egg, stir into flour mixture. Chill overnight or for several hours until stiff enough to roll. Using half at a time, roll to ⅛-inch thickness on a floured board, cut out with biscuit cutter. Sprinkle with hundreds and thousands and bake in a moderate oven (375° F. — Gas Mark 4) for 11 minutes or until lightly browned round the edges.

Variation:
Decorate cookies, after baking, with a mixture of icing sugar and water, blended to a smooth paste. Colouring may be added.

Orange biscuits *(Jamaica)*

2 eggs
5 oz. castor sugar
4 oz. flour

1 tablespoon nuts,
   finely chopped
rind of 3 oranges,
   finely grated

Beat eggs and gradually add sugar, beating until smooth and creamy. Fold in sifted flour, lightly fold in nuts and grated rinds. Spread mixture in a shallow, greased pan and bake in a moderate hot oven (375° F. — Gas Mark 4) for 35 minutes. While still hot, cut into thin sticks and leave in the pan to cool.

Note:
These biscuits may be served with a fruit salad or fruit jelly.

Orange cake *(Bahamas)*

4 oz. butter
8 oz. sugar
2 eggs
8 oz. flour
pinch salt
8 tablespoons sour milk
1 teaspoon baking soda

rind of 1 orange
2 tablespoons nuts,
  chopped
2 tablespoons raisins,
  chopped
juice of 2 oranges

Cream butter and sugar until light and fluffy, then beat in eggs, one at a time. Sift flour and salt and mix milk and baking soda. Add these alternately to creamed mixture, a little at a time, blending lightly and thoroughly. Pound together the orange rind, nuts and raisins and stir into cake mixture. Turn into a cake tin lined with greaseproof paper and bake for 35 minutes in a very moderate oven (350° F. — Gas Mark 3). Turn on to a wire rack and, while still hot, gradually pour the orange juice over.

Orange loaf *(Bahamas)*

4 oz. butter
8 oz. soft brown sugar
rind of 1 orange, grated
3 eggs, separated
8 oz. flour

pinch salt
2 teaspoons baking
  powder
4 tablespoons orange
  juice

Beat butter and sugar until creamy and fluffy, beat in orange rind and egg yolks, one at a time. Sift flour, salt and baking powder and add to creamed mixture a little at a time, alternately with orange juice. Whisk egg whites until very stiff and carefully fold into well-blended mixture. Turn into a loaf tin lined with greaseproof paper and bake for 1 hour in a very moderate oven (350° F. — Gas Mark 3).

Orange sandwich cake

4 oz. butter
12 oz. sugar
3 eggs
12 oz. flour

2½ teaspoons baking
powder
pinch salt
scant ½ pint milk

For the filling:

4 oz. butter, warmed
1 lb. icing sugar
pinch salt
2 egg yolks

1 teaspoon orange rind,
finely grated
orange juice

Cream butter and sugar until light and fluffy. Beat in eggs, one at a time, thoroughly. Sift flour, baking powder and a good pinch of salt. Add to mixture a little at a time, alternately with the milk until a smooth creamy mixture. Stir lightly and divide between two well-greased 9-inch sandwich tins. Bake for 35 minutes in a very moderate oven (350° F. — Gas Mark 3). Cool on a wire rack.

Make the filling: Beat butter until light. Sift icing sugar and salt and add to butter a little at a time, alternately with egg yolks. Stir in orange rind and beat in about 2 tablespoons orange juice until the mixture is smooth and spreads firmly. Sandwich cakes together with the mixture.

Orange squares *(Bahamas)*

4 oz. butter	4 tablespoons coconut,
8 oz. soft brown sugar	freshly grated
6 oz. flour	1 teaspoon baking
2 eggs	powder
4 tablespoons walnuts,	few drops vanilla
chopped	pinch salt

For the frosting:

8 oz. icing sugar	hot water
juice and rind of 1 orange	

Cream butter with 1 tablespoon sugar and allow to stand overnight. Then add 4 oz. sifted flour, mixing thoroughly. Spread crumbs on a well-greased baking sheet and bake in a moderate oven (375° F. — Gas Mark 4) for 10 minutes. Put aside to cool. Beat eggs thoroughly, then stir in walnuts, coconut, baking powder, vanilla, salt, remaining sugar and flour and blend well. Spread over cooled crumbs and bake in a slow oven (275° F. — Gas Mark 1) for 30 minutes.
Make the frosting: Beat icing sugar with orange juice, rind and enough very hot water to make a thick paste. Continue beating for a further 2 minutes, then spread on the cold cake. Cut into squares.

Peace 'n Plenty buns *(Exuma, Bahamas)*

2 lb. flour	1½ oz. yeast
1 oz. vegetable cooking oil	3 oz. sugar
1 teaspoon salt	warm water or milk

Combine flour, oil, salt, sugar and yeast, thoroughly. Mix to a stiff dough with warm water or milk and leave in a bowl, covered by a cloth, to rise for about ¾ hour in a warm room. Shape into about 20 buns, arrange on a well greased baking sheet. Bake in a moderate oven (375° F. — Gas Mark 4) for 30 minutes.

Alan, one of the chefs at the Club Peace 'n Plenty, gave me this recipe when we were sitting in the early morning sunshine overlooking the blue sea. In the distance, I could see Stocking Island across the Sound; below, little boats rocked gently on the waves. The Peace 'n Plenty is one of the small hotels on Great Exuma, the largest island in the Exuma chain and to my mind, quite the loveliest of the out-islands of the Bahamas. If you fancy retiring to the tropics, then Exuma may well be the place.

Peanut oaties *(Tortola, British Virgin Islands)*

4 oz. flour	1 egg, beaten
4 oz. sugar	4 oz. butter or margarine,
8 oz. oats	melted
4 oz. salted peanuts, crushed	1 tablespoon West India treacle

Sift flour, stir in sugar, oats and peanuts. Make a well in the centre and drop in the egg, butter or margarine and treacle. Mix well, gradually drawing down the dry ingredients. With a spoon, put small pats of mixture on a greased baking sheet and flatten with a fork until about ½-inch thick. Bake in a moderate oven (375° F. — Gas Mark 4) for about 30 minutes

Pineapple layer cake *(Bahamas)*

4 oz. butter
8 oz. sugar
7 oz. flour
1 teaspoon baking
  powder

pinch salt
6 tablespoons milk
1 teaspoon vanilla
  essence
3 egg whites
icing sugar, sifted

For the filling:

2 oz. flour
6 oz. sugar
pinch salt
¾ pint scalded milk

3 tablespoons pineapple,
  fresh or canned,
  finely chopped
3 egg yolks
1 tablespoon lemon
  or lime juice

Beat butter and 4 oz. sugar until light and fluffy. Sift flour, baking powder and salt; stir vanilla into milk. Add flour and milk to creamed mixture alternately, a little at a time, beating between each addition. Whisk egg whites until stiff and gradually add remaining sugar, beating all the time. Fold into cake mixture. Divide between 2 well-greased 7-inch sandwich tins and bake in a moderate oven (375°F. — Gas Mark 4) for 30 minutes. Turn on to a wire rack to cool.
Make the filling: Sift flour and stir in sugar and salt. Gradually add milk, stirring to keep mixture smooth. Cook over a low heat for 15 minutes, stirring. Remove from heat, stir in pineapple and allow to cool. When cool, add lightly beaten egg yolks and lemon or lime juice, then cook for a further 2 minutes. Allow to cool, then spread between cakes. Dust the top of the sandwich with icing sugar.

Planter's cake (*Jamaica*)

12 oz. butter
1¼ lb. icing sugar
9 eggs, separated

4 tablespoons strong
  black coffee
1 large sponge cake
  (see page 211)
3 tablespoons rum

Beat butter until very soft. Gradually beat in 1 lb. icing sugar and continue creaming until mixture is light and fluffy. Add egg yolks, one at a time, beating between each addition. Beat in coffee. Whisk egg whites until frothy and gradually add remaining sugar, beating until very stiff. Fold into creamed mixture. Slice sponge cake thinly and sprinkle with rum. Carefully sandwich cake together and coat top and sides with frosting. Chill thoroughly, for 3 hours, before serving.

Rum cake (*Netherlands Antilles*)

8 oz. butter
12 oz. sugar
6 eggs
juice and rind of 3 lemons
  or 4 limes
6 oz. flour

4 oz. cornmeal
2 teaspoons baking
  powder
3 tablespoons rum
4 oz. dessert chocolate,
  grated

Cream butter and sugar until light and fluffy. Beat in eggs, one at a time, then lemon juice and peel. Beat thoroughly. Sift flour with cornmeal, add baking powder and fold into creamed mixture, blending well but lightly. Stir in rum.
Bake in a large, shallow baking dish, well-greased, in a moderate oven (375° F. — Gas Mark 4) for 1 hour.
Sprinkle top with the grated chocolate and place under a hot grill for about 2 minutes when the chocolate should begin to melt. Quickly run a fork over it to spread and lift it in tiny peaks.

Rum snaps *(Jamaica)*

3½ oz. castor sugar
4 oz. butter
2 tablespoons molasses
  or golden syrup
3½ oz. flour

1½ teaspoons ground
  ginger
½ teaspoon lemon or
  lime juice
2 teaspoons Jamaica rum

For the filling:

thick cream

few drops rum

Melt sugar, butter and syrup together over a low heat,
stirring. Allow to cool. Sift flour and ginger. Stir lemon or
lime juice and rum into cooled syrup, then beat into dry
ingredients. Beat thoroughly. Using a teaspoon, drop small
blobs of mixture on to a greased baking sheet, leaving plenty
of space between. Spread each blob thinly with a wet finger
and bake in a very moderate oven (350° F. — Gas Mark 3)
for about 5 minutes. Allow to cool for a few seconds, lift with
a palette knife and shape by wrapping round the greased
handle of a wooden spoon. Allow to cool then slip from
handle. Fill with cream whipped with rum.

Note:

The secret of making good snaps is to cook only a few at
a time and to have several wooden spoon handles greased in
advance. Speed is essential.

Spiced date cake *(Bahamas)*

4 oz. butter
8 oz. sugar
2 eggs
8 oz. flour
3 teaspoons baking
    powder
1 teaspoon cinnamon,
    ground
1 teaspoon nutmeg,
    grated

1 teaspoon cloves,
    ground
pinch salt
6 tablespoons milk
3 tablespoons dates,
    chopped
1½ tablespoons nuts,
    chopped

Cream butter and sugar until light and fluffy. Beat in eggs, one at a time. Sift flour with baking powder, cinnamon, nutmeg, cloves and salt. Add to mixture a little at a time, alternately with milk. Mix dates with a little flour to separate them. Stir in dates and nuts, blending thoroughly. Divide between two well-greased 8-inch sandwich tins, and bake for 25 minutes in a moderate oven (375°F. — Gas Mark 4).

Sponge cake

4 eggs, separated
5 oz. castor sugar

1 lemon or 2 lime
    rinds, grated
5 oz. flour

Beat yolks with sugar in a warmed basin until thick, add rinds and beat again. Whisk egg whites until stiff and standing in peaks, then fold lightly into yolks and sugar. Sieve in flour and mix lightly with a wooden spoon. Grease a cake tin (10 ins. × 7½ ins.), dust with castor sugar and flour, pour mixture in. Bake in a moderately hot oven (400°F. — Gas Mark 5) for 30 minutes.

Tomato spice cake *(Bahamas)*

4 oz. butter
4 oz. soft brown sugar
4 oz. white sugar
2 eggs
6 tablespoons condensed tomato soup
8 oz. flour
½ teaspoon nutmeg, grated
½ teaspoon cloves, ground
½ teaspoon cinnamon, powdered
2 teaspoons baking powder
1 tablespoon nuts,
1 tablespoon raisins, chopped

Cream butter and sugars thoroughly, beat in eggs, one at a time. Gradually add tomato soup, beating between each addition. Sift flour with nutmeg, cloves, cinnamon and baking powder and fold into creamed mixture, blending carefully. Stir in nuts and raisins and turn into a well greased cake tin. Bake in a moderate oven (375° F. — Gas Mark 4) for 45 minutes — 1 hour.

Treacle biscuits *(Barbados)*

8 oz. flour
4 oz. castor sugar
3 oz. butter
6 oz. West India treacle

Sift flour, stir in sugar, then rub in butter. Make a well in the centre and pour in warmed treacle, then gradually stir in the dry ingredients, drawing down from the sides of the bowl. Turn on to a floured board and roll out thinly. Cut into rounds and bake on a greased baking sheet in a slow oven (300° F. — Gas Mark 2) for 30 minutes.

Treacle cake *(Barbados)*

12 oz. flour
1 teaspoon baking
powder
½ teaspoon bicarbonate of
soda
6 oz. butter

6 oz. soft brown sugar
8 oz. raisins, chopped
2 tablespoons West
India treacle
milk

Sift flour, baking powder and bicarbonate of soda, then rub butter in. Stir in sugar and raisins, then treacle. Mix to a dropping consistency with milk and turn into a 11½ ins. × × 8½ ins. cake tin lined with greaseproof paper. Bake in a moderate oven (375° F. — Gas Mark 4) for about 1¼ hours.

Treacle sponge *(Barbados)*

1½ oz. butter
2 oz. sugar
1 egg
4 oz. West India
treacle
4 oz. golden syrup

6 oz. flour
1 teaspoon mixed spice
1 teaspoon ginger,
ground
1 teaspoon baking soda
¼ pint hot water

For the filling:

2 oz. butter
4 oz. icing sugar
pinch ginger, ground

pinch cinnamon, ground
pinch mixed spice
1 teaspoon West India
treacle

Cream butter and sugar, beat in egg, warmed treacle and syrup. Sift flour with spices and soda and add to mixteure a little at a time, alternately with water. Turn into 2 well greased sandwich tins (9 ins. × 3 ins.) and bake in a moderate oven (375° F. — Gas Mark 4) for 20 minutes.
Make the filling: beat butter and gradually beat in icing sugar sifted with the ginger, cinnamon and mixed spice. Beat in treacle and continue beating until filling spreads smoothly. Sandwich cakes, when cool, with this.

Walnut cake *(Tobago)*

3 oz. butter
3 oz. castor sugar
2 tablespoons West India
  treacle
1 egg, lightly beaten

4 oz. flour
½ teaspoon baking
  soda
1 tablespoon walnuts,
  chopped

Cream the butter and sugar and beat in the warmed treacle. Add the egg, a little at a time, alternately with the flour and baking soda sifted together. Blend thoroughly and stir in the nuts. Bake in a well-greased sandwich tin in a moderately hot oven (375° F. — Gas Mark 5) for about 30 minutes

Note:

The cake may be decorated with this coffee butter icing.

1½ oz. butter
4 oz. icing sugar

2 teaspoons coffee
  essence
hot water

Cream butter and sugar, beat in essence and continue beating, adding a little hot water, to make a smooth paste. Spread on the cake.

Jams, chutneys, preserves and confectionery

On all the islands where citrus fruit grows, marmalade is made. Yet no book of Caribbean cookery would be complete without guava jam and cheese.

Citrus peel, candied and dried in the sun is luscious, much nicer than any sweetmeat; candied mint is something that can be made in many parts of the world. The melon rind recipes are economical; serve the melon as a cocktail or use one of the melon and rum recipes, cutting off the rind first and using it in one of the ways suggested.

Fresh nutmeg recipes can only be made where it grows, but could not be left out, green mangoes too, must be found where the cook lives, but this could be in almost any tropical place; papaya, or paw-paw, makes a very cheap preserve which is considered a good digestive. Sweets are made all through the islands, but on many, the children have a natural form of sweet in sugar cane, which they chew going home from school.

Banana-plus chutney *(St. Lucia)*

12 bananas	1 teaspoon allspice
1 lb. dates, pitted	2 teaspoons curry powder
1 lb. cooking apples, peeled and cored	2 tablespoons salt
2 lb. Spanish onions	1 pint malt vinegar
4 oz. crystallised ginger, chopped	1 lb. West India treacle
	½ pint water

Peel and chop bananas, chop dates and thinly slice apples and onions. Stir in ginger, allspice, curry powder, vinegar, treacle and water. Stir thoroughly. Turn into a lipped casserole and cook in a slow oven (275° F. — Gas Mark 1) for 2 hours. While still hot, bottle and seal.

Bay grape jelly *(Bermuda)*

7 lb. bay grapes,* equal measures of ripe and green	7 pints water sugar

Add grapes to water and bring to the boil, stirring with a wooden spoon and mashing the fruit as it softens. Boil for 10 minutes, then drip through a jelly bag without squeezing. Measure the juice and for every measuring jug of liquid, add an equal amount of sugar. Bring to the boil, stirring. Boil for about 15 minutes, skimming frequently, then continue boiling until a little tested on a plate will jell nicely. Pour into jars and allow to cool and set before sealing.

* Bay grapes are found by the sea on many of the Caribbean Islands. They are completely different both in taste and appearance from the European grape, but this recipe makes a very pleasant preserve when vine grapes are used. A squeeze of lemon adds to the flavour.

Bird pepper sherry *(Bermuda)*

bird peppers*   cooking sherry

Half fill a bottle with the peppers, left whole, and top with sherry. Allow to stand for 2 days before using.

* These peppers are small, very hot and red. As this condiment is used, top with sherry. After second topping up, discard peppers and make afresh.

Carrot jam *(Bermuda)*

4 lb. carrots   2½ lb. sugar
juice of 4 lemons

Wash and scrape carrots, grate finely, add lemon juice and sugar. Cook slowly over a very low heat until the preserve thickens. Pot and seal while hot.

Candied citrus peel *(Jamaica)*

peel of 2 oranges or   4 oz. sugar
 1 grapefruit   water

Cut fruit peel into strips, cover with cold water, bring to boil slowly; boil until tender.
Make a syrup with sugar and 4 tablespoons water; drop peel in, boil until nearly all is absorbed and peel is nearly transparent. Dry slowly in the sun or a warm, not hot, oven. The peel should be crystalline when quite dry.

Note:
Choose ripe, but not over-ripe fruit.

Candied mint leaves *(Bahamas)*

fresh mint, washed and
dried
white of 1 egg, lightly
beaten

6 drops oil of
peppermint
4 oz. granulated sugar

Paint mint leaves with egg white, mix peppermint oil with sugar. Dip each leaf into the flavoured sugar, coating each side. Place on waxed paper and dry in the sun or a warm place.

Note:

Use the mint leaves as a garnish for fruit salads. Gum arabic, 1 oz. to 1½ oz. water, can be used instead of white of egg.

Cherry jam *(Bahamas)*

cherries

sugar

Stone the cherries and weigh the pulp. To each 1 lb. fruit pulp add 1 lb. sugar, sprinkling in layers between the fruit. Cover the pot with a cloth and leave to stand overnight. Turn into a strong saucepan and bring to the boil, stirring. Simmer gently until jam is smooth and thick. Put into clean warmed jars and seal.

Coconut candy *(Jamaica)*

1 lb. granulated sugar
¼ pint water

8 oz. grated coconut
colouring (optional)

Boil sugar and water together until it forms a soft ball when dropped into cold water. Remove from heat and beat until cloudy and slightly granular, then stir in coconut. Grease a tin about 1½ ins. deep, pour in half the mixture when it cools a little. Colour the other half and smooth over the first half. When cool, but before it becomes hard, cut into squares.

Cucumber pickle *(Bermuda)*

4 lb. cucumbers	8 oz. coarse salt
1½ lb. onions, sliced	water
	vinegar

For spiced vinegar:

2 lb. soft brown sugar	4 teaspoons mixed
1½ pints cider vinegar	pickling spice
1 teaspoon celery salt	½ pint water

Put the coarsely sliced cucumbers and onions in separate crocks. Dissolve salt in 3½ pints water, pouring half over the cucumbers and half over the onions. Stand for about 12 hours. Drain thoroughly and turn both into a large saucepan. Cover with a solution made from equal quantities of vinegar and water, bring to almost boiling point and allow to simmer gently, never boiling, for 10 minutes, when the vegetables should be just tender, but not soft.

To spice vinegar: combine sugar, cider, vinegar, celery, salt, pickling spices and water. Bring to boil. Drain and pack the vegetables into jars, pour hot syrup over. Seal immediately.

A quick method:
Peel cucumbers and onions and slice both thinly. Cover with vinegar, to which salt and pepper has been added. Chill, and keep in the refrigerator.

Gooseberry jam *(Bahamas)*

gooseberries	sugar
salt water	water

Soak gooseberries for 12 hours in salt water (1 tablespoon salt to each pint of water). Drain and weigh the fruit, adding 1 lb. sugar to each pound soaked gooseberries. Add just enough water to cover fruit and bring to the boil. Boil until jam is thick and sets when tested. Bottle and seal while hot.

Green tomato pickle *(Bahamas)*

24 green tomatoes	salt water
8 onions	2 pints vinegar
8 green peppers	2 tablespoons whole allspice

Wash tomatoes, peel onions and remove seeds and pith from peppers. Slice all vegetables very finely, cover with salt water (1 tablespoon salt to each pint water) and stand for about 12 hours. Drain thoroughly, add vinegar, and spices tied in a muslin bag and bring to the boil. Simmer gently for 25 minutes. Pot and seal while hot.

Guava cheese *(Jamaica)*

ripe guavas	icing sugar
sugar	

Wash and peel guavas and rub through a sieve. Weigh pulp and add equal quantity of sugar. Boil until mixture shrinks from the sides of the pan, stirring all the time. When a little forms a ball if dropped into cold water, pour into a shallow greased dish. Cut into squares when firm and toss in icing sugar.

Guava jam *(Haiti)*

5 lb. guavas	4 oz. grated lemon or lime rind
water	4 lb. honey

Stone fruit and cook in a little water until soft. Strain and mix with rind and honey. Cook very slowly until thick. Allow to cool before putting into jars and sealing.

Mango chutney *(Jamaica)*

8 lb. green mangoes
5 pints vinegar, preferably Picapepper cane vinegar
brown sugar (same weight as mangoes *after* peeling and stoning)
4 oz. peeled green ginger or root ginger
1 oz. chillies
2 lb. raisins, seedless

Peel, stone and chop mangoes, boil with a little water until tender. Meanwhile, stir 4 pints vinegar and the sugar, bring to the boil and simmer until syrupy. Mince or chop ginger and chillies, moisten with remaining vinegar. Stir into the syrup, add raisins and cooked mangoes. Boil for 15 minutes, stirring all the time. Cool and bottle.

Marmalade *(Bermuda)*

2 lb. bitter oranges
4½ pints water
sugar
pinch salt

Wash and quarter the fruit, discard central cores and remove pips. Cover pips with ½ pint water and stand for 12 hours. Separate pulp from peel, mince the pulp and slice the peel. Weigh combined pulp and peel. Cover peel and pulp with remaining water and stand for 12 hours.
Bring fruit mixture to the boil and simmer until peel is tender. Bring pips to the boil and strain liquid into fruit mixture. Add sugar and equal weight of peel and pulp. Cook at a slow, rolling boil until a little will jell when tested on a plate. Skim while cooking to keep the marmalade clear.

Note:

Variations on this recipe are many. Use 1 grapefruit plus sufficient limes to make 2 lb. fruit; add 1 or 2 tangerines to bitter oranges; use 2 lb. limes instead of oranges; or make marmalade with 1 grapefruit, 1 orange and sufficient tangerines to make up to 2lb.

Mixed marmalade *(Bahamas)*

1 orange	1 1-lb. can pineapple
1 grapefruit	slices
1 lemon	4 pints water
	5 lb. sugar

Quarter fresh fruit and remove central cores, retain pips. Mince all fruit, including pineapple. Add water and pips tied in muslin and stand for 12 hours. Bring to the boil, simmer for 1 hour. Remove pips. Stir in sugar and boil slowly for 2 hours.

Note:
Though this marmalade jells nicely, it is not very stiff.

Nutmeg delight *(Grenada)*

nutmeg fruit	confectioner's sugar
sugar	

Cover fruit with boiling water and stand for 1 hour. Grate and weigh fruit and add equal weight of sugar. Bring to the boil, stirring constantly and boil until mixture leaves the bottom of the pan. Turn into a wet shallow dish and cool. Cut into squares, and roll in confectioner's sugar.

Nutmeg jelly *(Grenada)*

3 lb. nutmeg fruit	4 lb. sugar

Peel fruit and soak in water for 12 hours. Drain and cover with fresh water. Bring to the boil and simmer until soft. Strain, add sugar to the juice and boil slowly until a little jells when tested on a plate. Pot and seal while hot.

Old sour *(Bahamas)*

1 pint fresh lime juice	1 tablespoon salt

Strain lime juice, pour into a sterilized bottle, add salt and shake to dissolve. Stand at room temperature for at least 2 weeks to ferment, before using with fish or meat.

Note:
Old sour seasoning will keep indefinitely and to make it hotter, add a little ground Cayenne pepper before it ferments.

Orange cheese *(Trinidad)*

grated rind of 1 orange
3 oz. sugar
1 oz. butter
1 teaspoon lemon or
fresh lime juice

2 teaspoons orange juice
2 eggs, thoroughly
beaten

Mix orange rind and sugar and stand for about 15 minutes. Melt butter in a double saucepan, stir in rind, sugar, fruit juices and eggs, and cook gently until thickened, stirring frequently. Use as lemon cheese.

Orange toffee *(Jamaica)*

2 oz. butter
1 lb. granulated sugar

juice of ½ orange

Melt butter, stir in sugar and orange juice. Boil for 10 minutes stirring gently. Test by dropping into cold water when, if ready, it sets into a brittle strip. Pour into a greased tin, mark into squares when cool, but not hard.

Papaya lime marmalade *(Nevis)*

3 lb. papaya pulp*
¼ pint fresh lime or lemon
juice

1 tablespoon pineapple
juice
4 lb. honey

*Available, canned, at Oriental stores

Sieve papaya pulp, mix with fruit juices and honey. Stir over a slow heat, using an asbestos mat to prevent burning, until the mixture thickens. Put into jars and seal.

Pineapple jam *(Bahamas)*

pineapple   sugar

Peel pineapple and grate fruit finely. To each lb. pulp add ¾ lb. sugar. Bring to the boil, stirring. Stir until jam jells when a little is dropped on to a cold plate. Pot and seal while hot.

Pineapple fudge *(Jamaica)*

1 fresh pineapple or   1 lb. granulated sugar
  1 1-lb can pineapple,
  drained

Peel and grate fruit. Add sugar, heat slowly until dissolved. Boil fast until syrup sets when put on a cool plate. Beat for 5 minutes, pour into a greased tin. Cut when cold.

Pumpkin preserve *(Bahamas)*

3 lb. pumpkin   1 orange
2 lb. sugar   pinch salt
1 lemon or 2 limes

Peel and cut pumpkin into ¼-inch thick slices, then chop them across and pack into a large jar. Add sugar, cover and stand for at least 12 hours. Drain liquid from pumpkin and bring this to the boil. Boil until syrup is thick. Add pumpkin and lemon or lime and orange, sliced thinly. Stir in salt, bring to the boil. Cook until thick and clear. Pot and seal.

Spiced watermelon rind *(Bahamas)*

2 lb. watermelon rind   1 lemon or 2 limes,
salt   sliced
water   1 stick cinnamon
1 pint vinegar   1 teaspoon whole cloves
¾ pint water   1 teaspoon whole
2 lb. sugar   allspice

Remove all flesh from the rind, cut into pieces and soak for about 12 hours in a salt solution (1 tablespoon salt to each pint water). Drain and cook gently in fresh water until tender. Turn into preserving pan, add vinegar, water, sugar and lemon, or lime finely sliced. Tie spices in a muslin bag, add to pan, and bring to the boil, stirring. Simmer gently until clear and transparent. Pack the rind into jars, fill to overflowing with syrup and seal immediately.

Sweet pickled watermelon rind *(Bermuda)*

rind of 1 medium-sized watermelon	4 tablespoons whole cloves
8 lb. sugar	4 tablespoons cinnamon sticks
1¾ pint vinegar	

Trim outer skin and flesh from watermelon rind, chop into small pieces, cover with water and simmer until tender. Boil together sugar and vinegar with cloves and cinnamon sticks tied in muslin. Boil for 10 minutes, gently. Add tender rind and simmer over a low heat until clear and transparent. Pack into jars, fill to overflowing with syrup and tightly seal immediately.

Sweet pickled peppers *(Bahamas)*

12 red peppers	1 teaspoon whole allspice
12 green peppers	
18 small onions	1 teaspoon celery salt
1¼ lb. soft brown sugar	2 tablespoons salt
1½ pints water	

Remove seeds and pith from peppers and mince coarsely. Cover with boiling water, stand for 5 minutes, and drain. Mince onions coarsely and add, with their juice, to peppers. Stir in sugar and water, add spices, tied in a muslin bag, and salt to taste. Bring to the boil and simmer gently for about 45 minutes — 1 hour. Pot and seal at once.

Tomato jam *(Bermuda)*

5 lb. tomatoes
sugar

3 tablespoons green
ginger, finely grated

Peel and core tomatoes, then thinly slice. Weigh them and add equal amount of sugar. Stir in ginger and turn into a strong saucepan. Stand over a very low heat until juice begins to flow. Bring to the boil and simmer gently, stirring all the time, for about 20 minutes, when the jam should be thick and clear. Turn into warmed jars and seal immediately.

Treacle marmalade

1 lb. bitter oranges
1 lemon or 2 limes
3½ pints water

3 lb. sugar
2 oz. West India treacle

Peel oranges and lemon or lime and slice very finely. Chop pulp, discarding central cores and putting pips into a muslin bag. Cook fruit, peel and pips in water for about 3 hours over a low heat. Remove pips, stir in sugar and treacle and boil hard for about 1 hour, until a little sets when tested on a plate. Pot and seal.

West Indies chutney

2 lb. cooking apples
8 oz. onions
4 oz. soft brown sugar
1 teaspoon salt
½ tablespoon mixed
  pickling spice

½ teaspoon ground
  ginger
½ pint vinegar
6 oz. West India
  treacle

Peel and core apples, peel onions and finely chop both. Turn into a pan with remaining ingredients, stir thoroughly and bring to the boil, stirring. Simmer gently for 2 hours, without a lid, when chutney should be of a jammy consistency. Cool slightly before bottling and sealing.

Beverages, fruit and non-alcoholic drinks

In a hot climate it is essential to drink plenty, whether water, fruit juice or weak tea. In the Caribbean, where citrus abounds on many of the islands, fruit drinks are the most obvious choice. In Jamaica, for instance, there are little fruit juice bars outside several of the main shopping centres, "Jamaica Juices" they are called. Here one can buy cartons of fresh juice to carry home or have a drink on the spot. They sell the obvious citrus and pineapple drinks and also pawpaw and mango juice, cane syrup and sour sop juice.

Nearly every drink in the Islands is garnished by a thin slice of lime, balanced on the rim of the glass.

I learnt to make a very economical health drink in the West Indies from the peelings of melon or pineapple. Add a little sugar or glucose then steep peelings in boiling water before straining and chilling thoroughly in the refrigerator.

Banana chiffonade

6 servings:

4 ripe bananas, sliced	½ teaspoon almond
4 tablespoons honey	flavouring
1½ pints milk	nutmeg
¼ teaspoon vanilla essence	

Blend all ingredients except nutmeg in an electric mixer. Chill thoroughly and serve in frosted glasses sprinkled with nutmeg.

Bentley, a children's cocktail *(Antigua)*

1 oz. sugar	soda water
1½ tablespoons water	dash Angostura bitters
1½ tablespoons fresh lime or lemon juice	cherries

Boil the sugar and water to make a syrup. Cool, then chill. When required, add fruit juice and soda water to taste, according to whether a long or short drink is desired. Just before serving, add a dash of Angostura bitters, some crushed ice and top each glass with a cherry.

Cherry juice *(Bahamas)*

cherries, well ripened	castor sugar

Extract stones then crush cherries thoroughly. Squeeze through muslin and collect juice. Sweeten to taste and chill thoroughly before serving.

Citrus syrup

freshly squeezed citrus fruit juice	sugar water

Measure fruit juice. Make an equal quantity of syrup with sugar and water, using 2 parts sugar to 1 part water. Add fruit juice to syrup, bring just to the boil and pour into warmed, sterilized bottles. Seal while hot. Dilute with 2 tablespoons syrup to each ½ pint water when serving.

Note:
Citrus syrup will keep for about 6 months and can be used, diluted, as required.

Coral Island nectar *(Barbados)*

2–3 servings:

juice of 4 oranges juice of 1 lemon or 2 limes	½ pint apricot pulp, sieved (peach pulp may be used) 1 pint water

Shake all ingredients together until blended, or blend in an electric mixer. Chill and serve.

Hangover healer *(Bahamas)*

1 serving:

1 teaspoon vinegar 2 teaspoons Worcestershire sauce	salt pepper 1 egg

Mix vinegar and sauce in a glass, add a tiny sprinkling of salt and pepper and drop in the egg, taking care not to break the yolk. The mixture is swallowed without breaking the yolk.

Iced coffee

4–6 servings:

2 pints water   cream, (optional)
8 tablespoons coffee,
   freshly ground

Pour boiling water over coffee grounds in a warm jug. Leave to stand for 4 minutes, stir and stand for 1 minute. Strain into a jug and chill. Serve black or with cream.

Note
Coffee for iced coffee is made rather stronger than usual because it tends to lose some of its flavour when chilled.

Mixed fruit cordial *(Trinidad)*

4–6 servings:

6 tablespoons sugar   juice of 2 grapefruit
6 tablespoons water   iced water or iced soda
juice of 4 large oranges   water
juice of 2 lemons   lemon or lime slices

Boil sugar and water for 2 minutes, then allow to cool. Strain fruit juices and chill for at least 2 hours. Sweeten to taste with syrup and dilute with plain or soda water. Serve in glasses with frosted rims and decorate with lemon or lime slices.

Orange milk

4 servings:

1½ pints milk   ½ pint orange juice,
                                 freshly squeezed

Chill ingredients separately and pour milk into the glasses on top of the orange juice.

Papaya mango cocktail

⅓ papaya juice
⅓ mango juice

⅓ lemon or lime juice
honey
cherries to decorate

Mix all juices, preferably in an electric blender. Sweeten with honey to taste, blend again and chill slightly. Serve each glass decorated with a cherry on a stick.

Note:
This cocktail, high in digestive enzymes, is known as an antidote to over-eating and is served at Christmas in some of the Leeward Islands.

Pineapple drink

peelings from 1 pineapple
2 cloves
1 small piece dried orange
   peel (optional)

2 pints water
sugar to taste

Drop peelings, cloves and orange peel into a large jug. Bring water to the boil and pour over contents of the jug. Cover and allow to stand for 1 day. Strain and sweeten to taste before serving or bottling.

Note:
This drink will keep for 2–3 days.

Spiced tea *(Grenada)*

3 or 4 blades mace,
according to strength
desired

½ pint water
nutmeg, grated
sugar to taste

Boil mace in water for 15 minutes. Strain, add sugar to liquid and serve with sprinkling of nutmeg.
Serve very hot as a warming drink to give relief from colds, influenza etc.
Variations:
Rum, milk or cream can be added.

Vigger-viver

2 parts fresh orange juice
1 part fresh grapefruit juice

honey to taste

Blend juices and stir in enough honey to sweeten slightly. Chill before serving.

Drinks, cocktails and home-made wines

Rum, the drink of the people in the West Indies, is 'the spirit of sugar'. This was the official definition in 1909; previously it had such names as 'Kill-Devil' in 1647, 'Rumbullion' in 1650 ("the chief fuddling they make on the island of Rumbullion" is how an old book on Barbados describes it). Finally, in 1661 this name was abbreviated to rum and so it has remained.

Fermented molasses, or cane juice, is distilled to make rum, re-distilled it becomes spirits of wine. There are three main types, Bacardi, a light, brandy type which originated in Cuba, but is now made in the Bahamas and Puerto Rico as well as in Spain, Mexico and Brazil.

Demerara rum is darker than Bacardi, a medium type; watch your step if you drink it, there can be as much as 80% alcohol content. This type comes from Barbados, Haiti and St. Croix. Jamaica rum, the third type, is dark and richly flavoured.

In this chapter there are recipes for local brews, mawby, a kind of beer made from tree bark, sorrel, ginger beer, the Christmas drink of Trinidad and a far cry from those innocuous stone bottles we had as schoolchildren.

After-deck special

2 parts gin	dash tomato juice
1 part Cointreau	crushed ice
1 part lemon or lime juice	

Shake all ingredients well together.

Around the world in 80 days

1 tablespoon fresh lemon or lime juice	½ tablespoon Bacardi rum
1 tablespoon white Crème de Cacao	½ tablespoon Jamaica rum
	1 tablespoon Barbados rum
	crushed ice

Shake all ingredients well together.

Bacardi planter's punch

2 oz. Bacardi rum	1 slice orange
1 teaspoon sugar	cherry
1 tablespoon fresh lemon or lime juice	pineapple
crushed ice	mint

Stir rum, sugar and lemon or lime juice well together. Pour into a large glass filled with crushed ice. Garnish with an orange slice, a cherry, a cube of fresh pineapple and plenty of mint.

Big bamboo

3 parts port
1 part sweet Vermouth

2 dashes Orange Curaçao
crushed ice

Shake all ingredients vigorously together.

Egg and rum drink

1 egg
1 tablespoon rum

1 teaspoon sugar
¼ pint milk

Break egg into a basin and add rum and sugar, beating vigorously until thoroughly blended. Heat milk to almost boiling and pour on to egg mixture, stirring all the time. Strain into a warmed mug and serve hot.

Egg and rum flip

1 egg
1 teaspoon sugar

1 teaspoon rum
¼ pint milk

Separate the egg. Cream yolk thoroughly with sugar. Add rum and milk. Whip white stiffly and fold in. Serve chilled.

Empire top

2 parts rum
1 part French Vermouth
1 part Grand Marnier

1 dash Angostura bitters
crushed ice

Shake all ingredients well together.

Fly *(British Guiana)*

1 lb. white sweet potatoes	3–4 lb. sugar
4 large limes, or 3 lemons	1 egg white, well beaten
½ oz. cloves	water
½ oz. mace	

Peel and grate potato and wash until free of starch. Squeeze limes or lemons and strain juice. Bring clove and mace to the boil in a little water and strain. Pack potato into a stone jar, add sugar, lime juice and cooled mace and clove liquid. Add 1 gallon water and stir until sugar is dissolved. Whisk in egg white, cover and allow to stand for 8 days.

Strain and bottle in strong dark bottles, tying down the corks.

Note:

This may be used after 4 days but it is much better when more mature.

Ginger beer *(Trinidad)*

2 oz. green ginger	2 oz. cream of tartar
1 gallon boiling water	¾ oz. brewers' yeast,
juice and rind of 2 small	dissolved in a little
limes or lemons	warm water
	1½ lb. sugar

Wash and pound ginger and pour boiling water over. Add juice and rind of limes and cream of tartar. Cover jar with several thicknesses of cloth, but stir frequently. When liquid is lukewarm, add dissolved yeast and stir very well. Cover again and allow to stand for 6 hours. Stir in sugar until dissolved, then bottle.

Allow to stand for at least 3 or 4 days before using.

Note:

Caribbean cooks add a dash of rum to their home-made ginger beer to make it keep better.

This is *the* Christmas drink in Trinidad.

Ginger wine *(British Guiana)*

1 lb. raisins	2½ lb. Demerara sugar
2 oz. ginger, well bruised	3 limes or 2 lemons,
1 gallon water	peeled and thinly sliced

Add raisins and ginger to water and bring to the boil. Boil
for 30 minutes. Pour on to sugar and lemons and stir. Cool,
strain into a jar and cover.
It will be ready for use in a week.

Hibiscus *(Bahamas)*

1 tablespoon fresh lemon or lime juice	½ tablespoon Pimms No. 1 Cup
1 tablespoon fresh orange juice	2 tablespoons light rum crushed ice
1 tablespoon pineapple juice	

Shake all ingredients together thoroughly.

Jamaica rumlet

1 measure light Jamaica rum	¼ measure dry vermouth cracked ice

Stir ingredients well together.

Jamaica juicer

1 part rum	crushed ice
1 part fresh orange juice	slice of fresh lime
1 part fresh pineapple juice	or lemon

Shake rum and fruit juices vigorously with ice. Strain over
lime or lemon.

Mawby *(British Guiana)*

1 heaped tablespoon
mawby bark
1 small strip dried orange
peel
½ ins. strip cinnamon

3–4 cloves
blade mace
6½ pints cold water
1 lb. sugar

Boil mawby and orange with cinnamon, cloves and mace in ½ pint water till strong tea results, taking about 5 minutes. Allow to cool, then add sugar and remaining water. Do not skimp the sugar as the drink loses its sweetness during fermentation. Strain into bottles, filling to the shoulder only, leaving the entire neck free for the froth. Screw down and leave for 3–4 days.

Montagu 'High' *(Montagu Beach Hotel, Nassau)*

1 part gin
1 part French Vermouth
1 part lemon or lime juice

2 dashes Benedictine
2 dashes Grand Marnier
crushed ice

Shake all ingredients vigorously together.

Nassau cocktail

1 part lemon or lime juice
1 part Crème de Cacao

3 parts light rum
crushed ice

Shake all ingredients together vigorously.

Nassau pick-up

2 parts brandy
1 part Martini Vermouth

1 part port
crushed ice

Shake all ingredients vigorously together.

Orange blossom cocktail *(Bahamas)*

1 part orange juice,
freshly squeezed

1 part dry gin
crushed ice

Shake ingredients well together. Strain into a glass.

Orange Collins

4 servings:

8 lumps sugar
4 oranges
Angostura bitters
8 teaspoons water

8 tablespoons gin
ice cubes
soda water
4 sprigs borage or mint

Rub sugar lumps over orange peel and put 2 lumps into the bottom of each tall glass. Add a dash of Angostura bitters and 2 teaspoons water to each glass, the 2 tablespoons gin and juice of 1 orange. Add 4 or 5 ice cubes to each drink and stir until the glasses frost. Top with soda water and decorate with borage or mint.

Orange wine *(Jamaica)*

4 quarts orange juice
1 quart lime or lemon juice
3 lb. brown sugar
2 quarts strong dark rum

2 tablespoons unslaked
lime
½ pint milk

Mix together orange and lime or lemon juice, sugar and rum. Stand 3 days in a stone crock or jar. Add lime and milk, mixing well. Allow to stand another 4 days. Strain and bottle.

Note:
White egg shells can be used in place of lime to clear the wine.

Ponce de crème *(Martinique)*

½ medium can
unsweetened condensed
milk
¼ pint rum
3 eggs
sugar to taste

vanilla essence to taste
few drops lime or lemon
juice
ice
Angostura or nutmeg

Add milk, rum and eggs to sugar, essence and juice, beat lightly. Add crushed ice and sprinkle with Angostura or grated nutmeg.

Note:

Serve as a dessert or a drink.

Poor man's liqueur

1 bottle rum
1 tablespoon sugar

rind of 1 orange
rind of 1 lemon or 2 limes

Pour a little rum into a large bowl and stir in sugar. Add whole rind of orange and lemon and beat with a spoon to extract juices. Add remaining rum and set alight. Stir with a fork until flame turns from blue to yellow. Extinguish by putting a plate over the bowl. Serve with a lipped ladle into liqueur glasses.

Note:

This was the late Ian Fleming's recipe for poor man's liqueur and, he warned, it is very potent.

Planter's punch, Bahamas style

1 tablespoon lemon juice
1 tablespoon orange juice
1 tablespoon pineapple
juice

½ tablespoon grenadine
2 tablespoons rum
shaved ice

Shake all ingredients together vigorously.

Planter's punch, Bermuda style

½ teaspoon sugar
1 tablespoon lemon or lime
  juice
1 tablespoon pineapple
  juice
½ oz. falernum (sugar
  syrup, page 243)
1 tablespoon Barbados rum
1 tablespoon Jamaica rum

½ tablespoon Demerara
  rum
½ tablespoon grenadine
2 dashes Angostura bitters
shaved ice
2 ice cubes
½ slice orange
½ slice lemon or lime
1 maraschino cherry

Shake well together sugar, lemon juice, pineapple juice, falernum, rums, grenadine, bitters and shaved ice. Pour over ice cubes and garnish with orange, lemon and cherry.

Planter's Punch, Jamaica style

1 part fresh lime or lemon
  juice
2 parts sugar
3 parts dark rum

4 parts crushed ice
dash Angostura bitters
maraschino cherries to
  decorate

Shake lime juice, sugar, rum, ice and bitters vigorously, pour into tall glasses and garnish each with a cherry.

Rice wine *(Jamaica)*

1 lb. rice, unwashed
3 lb. brown sugar
1 lb. raisins, seedless
8 oz. prunes, chopped and
  stoned

½ an orange, sliced
12 oz. yeast
3 quarts water

Put the rice in a big jar. Add sugar, raisins, prunes and orange. Melt yeast in a little cold water, add to jar. Bring water to the boil, pour into jar and close tightly.
Allow to stand for 3 weeks, shaking from time to time, but be careful to keep jar tightly closed.

Rum and honey *(Haiti)*

1 teaspoon honey, strained

2 oz. Jamaica rum
cracked ice

Dissolve honey in rum, stirring well. Turn into a glass with cracked ice and stir.

Rum beginning

3 tablespoons rum
3 teaspoons fresh lime or lemon juice

dash sweet Vermouth
crushed ice

Shake all ingredients well together.

Rum Collins *(Bermuda)*

3 ice cubes
1 tablespoon simple syrup*
1 tablespoon fresh lemon or lime

2 tablespoons Barbados rum
soda

Put ice cubes into a ½-pint glass and pour syrup, lemon juice and rum over. Top with soda, as you stir with a long spoon.

* Make by boiling equal quantities of sugar and water together until it forms a thick syrup.

Rum glorianna

2 tablespoons rum
2 teaspoons fresh lemon or lime juice

1 teaspoon apricot brandy
crushed ice

Shake all ingredients vigorously together.

Rum sour *(Bermuda)*

1½ tablespoons fresh lime
or lemon juice
2 tablespoons Barbados
rum

½ tablespoon falernum
(see below)
½ teaspoon sugar
crushed ice

Shake all ingredients well together. Strain into a whisky sour glass.

Rum swizzle *(Bermuda)*

1 teaspoon sugar
1½ tablespoons lime or
lemon juice
½ tablespoon falernum
(sugar syrup)*
dash Angostura bitters

1 tablespoon Barbados
rum
1 tablespoon Demerara
rum
shaved ice

Turn all ingredients into a wide-mouthed glass jug. Churn vigorously with a swizzle stick until jug begins to frost. Strain into a cocktail glass.

* Falernum is a sugar syrup with an almond essence made from the same sugar cane as rum.

Santiago nightcap

2 oz. Bacardi rum
2 teaspoons orange
Curaçao

yolk of 1 egg
cracked ice

Shake ingredients vigorously together with ice. Strain into a champagne glass.

September morn

2 oz. Bacardi rum
$\frac{1}{2}$ teaspoon sugar
2 teaspoons egg white
2 teaspoons raspberry syrup, or grenadine

juice of $\frac{1}{2}$ lemon, or 1 lime, strained
cracked ice

Shake all ingredients well with cracked ice and serve in a cocktail glass. Stick a straw to the lip of the glass.

Sorrel

1 lb. sorrel, seeded
$\frac{1}{2}$ square strip of ginger
1$\frac{1}{2}$ ins. strip dried orange peel
6 cloves

3 pints boiling water
1 lb. sugar
few grains rice or barley

Wash sorrel, removing all trace of seeds. Put in a stone jar with ginger, orange peel and cloves. Pour over water and allow to stand for 24 hours. Strain and add sugar. Pour into bottles adding a few grains of barley or rice to each to help fermentation. Stand for another 24–36 hours. Serve with ice.

Note:

There are two types of sorrel, red and white. White sorrel makes a more acid drink, so allow 1 extra pint water.

South Camp Road *(Kingston, Jamaica)*

3 oz. dry gin
1 teaspoon Grand Marnier
juice of $\frac{1}{2}$ lemon or 1 lime
dash Angostura bitters
dash orange bitters
3 oz. French vermouth

1 teaspoon Pernod or absinthe
1 egg white
$\frac{1}{2}$ teaspoon grenadine
2 teaspoons brown sugar
cracked ice

Shake all ingredients vigorously together. Serve in champagne glasses.

Velvet hammer *(Bermuda)*

¼ teaspoon sugar or lime
1 tablespoon lemon or
 lime juice
½ tablespoon falernum
 (see page 243)
1 teaspoon grenadine
1 tablespoon fresh
 pineapple juice

1 tablespoon dry sherry
1 tablespoon Barbados
 rum
1 tablespoon Demerara
 rum
½ tablespoon Jamaica rum
crushed ice

Shake all ingredients well together. Strain into whisky sour glasses.

Note:

This is a more concentrated version of the Bermuda Planter's punch and is served in smaller glasses.

Wedding rum punch *(Bermuda)*

25 servings:

scant ½ pint Grenadine
scant pint lemon juice
1 pint 6 oz. falernum
 (see page 243)
1 pint 6 oz. Barbados rum
1 pint 6 oz. Demerara rum

2 pints 6 oz. unsweetened
 pineapple juice, canned
10 dashes Angostura
 bitters
ice
orange slices
cucumber, sliced thinly

Stir all ingredients together in a large punch bowl with plenty of ice. Float thin slices of orange and cucumber on top to garnish.

Note:

To make a bubbly punch, use less ice and, just before serving, add plenty of well-chilled ginger ale.

Index of Recipes

249

251

254